OFFSHORE PURSUIT

A Guide to Fishing Atlantic Blue Water

By John Unkart

All illustrations by Heather Riser
Production by Kari Snyder

GEARED UP PUBLICATIONS, LLC
EDGEWATER, MD
WWW.GEAREDUPPUBLICATIONS.COM

This book is dedicated to my father, who always found the time and patience to take me fishing.

"Fishing success is found where skill, preparation and luck converge!" —Charlie Cooke

ACKNOWLEDGMENTS

I would like to thank the following people, many with whom I have fished with over the years and who selflessly contributed fishing techniques and information for use in this book.

Captain Ted Ohler
Captain Josh Rusky
Captain Willie Zimmerman
Captain Rob Skillman (www.endeavorsportfishing.com)
Captain Mark Radcliff (www.fishbonz.net)
Captain Ron Callis (www.reeladdiction.com)
Captain Cary Hanna (www.newlattitude.com)
Capt. John G. McMurray (www.nycflyfishing.com)
Capt. Scott Hamilton (www.flyfishingextremes.com)
Charles (Pop) Cooke
Tom Kessler
Lenny Rudow
Richard Ohanlon
Fred (Cuz) Unkart
Heather Riser (illustrations)

And a special thanks to my wife and family who tolerate my passion for fishing!

INTRODUCTION

The Atlantic waters off the coastline of the eastern United States offer the opportunity to participate in world-class offshore fishing. Pelagic species inhabiting the warm water of the Gulf Stream migrate from Florida to Long Island. Whether you call the blue water your fishing grounds or want to experience this exciting fishery for the first time, success should not be left to Lady Luck. Knowledge and experience are necessary to produce results.

This book teaches the proper techniques for catching fish offshore. Whether your challenge is to experience the thrilling aerial display of marlin, or cranking tilefish out of the depths along the 100-fathom line, the necessary information can be found between the covers of this book. Novices and seasoned offshore veterans will find new and innovative ways to increase hookups. Learn what each species prefers at the end of a line. Methods of trolling, types of spreads, how to chunk for tuna and when to use a kite to enhance catches are all covered in detail.

From rigging information to tips on how to fight trophy fish, it's all here in this one book, a guide to help bend rods on your Offshore Pursuits.

TABLE OF CONTENTS

— CHAPTER ONE —
BEGINNING THE ADVENTURE

Drastic changes have occurred in offshore fishing over the past 50 years. If you go back in offshore fishing history, at one time, participation required large and very expensive sportfishing boats. It was a brotherhood for those who could afford a luxury lifestyle. Images of Hemingway with rod in hand, standing next to the blue marlin he loved to pursue, surface to mind. Luckily for us today, advancements in technology have made it possible for the average family to participate in the one-time exclusive club of offshore fishing. Smaller, stronger manufactured hulls propelled by to-day's new powerplants place the far offshore waters within reach of all who dream of the ultimate fishing adventures.

It seems like every day newly developed items are released onto the fishing market to improve your chances of success. Of course, a boat

Fishing is fun! Marie (author's wife, left) and friend Paula enjoy a beautiful sunrise while running to the canyons for a day of billfishing.

has not been constructed large enough to carry everything available to "catch" fish! But, I have made the decision of what's necessary for offshore fishing a little easier. This chapter covers guidelines for safety and essential equipment for getting up and running in the exciting sport of offshore fishing. Additional chapters contain recommendations for terminal tackle, lures, bait and an examination of each species you are likely to encounter along with fishing tips, tricks and recommendations.

HOW MUCH BOAT IS ENOUGH?

After fishing in the Atlantic ocean for over 40 years, I can say with hesitation, "No boat is large enough... period." That is, until you pull up to the fuel dock! Offshore anglers must be conscience of one thought: safety can never be less then the first priority when the compass bearing is east. There is always a factor of risk when leaving an inlet, on a glass calm or rough day, with the intent of covering many miles of ocean in pursuit of fish.

My first "offshore" boat was under 20'. Certainly, it was not the boat I wanted or dreamed about when paging through boating magazines, but it was what I could afford. The boat's size did not deter me from following my dreams of fishing offshore. I was lucky and had a few close calls, but in the end, the multipurpose boat served me well for fishing the bays and out to the 20 fathom line of the Mid Atlantic, where I cut my teeth on offshore predators. The number of days spent offshore was limited only by the weather. Of course, most days were spent with an eye to the sky and a dedicated ear to the NOAA weather station, listening for any unexpected changes in the forecast. The weather is of major importance, so much in fact that a section of this book is dedicated to weather. And, there are other issues that need to be taken into account. The amount of usable gallons of fuel in the tank determines how far offshore you fish. Carrying extra fuel in portable cans and trying to refuel at sea is a safety issue and certainly not recommended. A major consideration to take into account, until you are familiar with how much fuel your boat burns per hour at cruising speed and trolling, is that a fuel gauge normally reads with the boat floating stationary on the water. When a boat is trolling with the bow slightly raised, the fuel gauge may show more fuel then what's in the tanks. Until it is learned how many gallons per hour are being consumed by the engine(s), do not trust the fuel gauges. The point is, so long as you stay within the limits of your boat's ability and do not push or exceed the boundaries you have set and are comfortable with, even a boat in the 20-something or longer range puts blue water within your grasp.

Safety is found in numbers. Join a fishing club and when possible, buddy up and run with another boat. At the very least, always leave an intended float plan. Inform family and friends, or if the boat is kept at a marina, leave information with the dock master of your intended fishing area and approximate return time. Try to stick with the plan. However, when the radio lights up and you decide to run 20 miles chasing a hot bite, make sure someone gets notified even if it necessitates a relayed radio message. If you fail to show up at the dock, your rescuers will appreciate having an idea of where to search for you—which can not compare with how happy you will be when found.

PREPARE FOR THE WORST

What can go wrong offshore? Broken fan belts, spark plugs blown out of the engine block, bent props, broken shafts, hooks in hands, steel leaders severing fingers, and heat stroke only touch the surface! Over the years, just about everything imaginable, outside of having a boat disappear from beneath me, has occurred while fishing offshore. The crew and I survived every mishap with only rattled nerves, bruised egos and short hospital stays. Being prepared for the unexpected got us through each of these mishaps. If you spend time offshore, sooner or later problems are going to occur.

You may be the captain, nonetheless, another person onboard needs to know how to operate the GPS, VHF radio, safety equipment, and the boat itself. In addition, the crew needs to know procedures for handling a man-overboard situation. This knowledge needs to be shared calmly before leaving the dock, not by yelling and shouting directions from in the water. By all means, suppress the urge to run offshore by yourself (if this occurs on a regular basis, consider seeking professional help—you may have social problems not addressed in this book).

In an emergency situation, such as a fire, life jackets need to be accessible. They are of no value in a locked compartment or belowdecks when everyone is abandoning ship. Technology has all but eliminated the "I'm not wearing one of those bulky life vests" excuse, with the new inflatable vests and belts. By all means, children and poor swimmers need to wear life jackets at all times.

Carry plenty of water; in case of a break down, it is essential. Also, having something to eat while drifting for hours and waiting for assistance does not hurt. MREs (meal's ready to eat) can be stored onboard for years and are very tasty, especially when near starvation.

If you have freezer space, freeze your own jugs of water instead of purchasing cubed/crushed ice. This will provide drinking water in emergencies as the jugs thaw. In addition, thawed jugs provide clean water to refill the freshwater cooling system after a hose blows, leaving your bilge full of antifreeze.

Carry a quality first aid kit, know what is in it and how to use the contents. Help is a long way off. You and everyone onboard are 911, the first responders. The Coast Guard chopper will seem to take hours just to fly 60 miles. You do not need to be an EMT, but basic knowledge in first aid treatment for burns, heavy bleeding, sunstroke, hypothermia, and reviving a person who nearly drowned, is imperative. If you are not comfortable in your level of proficiency for providing first aid, I strongly advise taking advantage of a Red Cross instructional class. Their website offers a zip code search for a course offered in or near your community. Check out www.redcross.org/services/hss/courses. Remember, when the %@$# hits the fan, everyone looks toward the captain to handle the situation. At the risk of sounding like a boy scout, be prepared, it may save someone's life.

Drink plenty of fluids on hot days and stay out of the blistering sun when possible, as heat stroke can sneak up on a person. Alcohol is not recommended since it can induce dehydration and impair judgment, not to mention possible prosecution for operating a vessel under the influence. There is plenty of time to celebrate the day's catch after hitting the dock.

It is surprising what can be fixed at sea. Taking a starter off to fix brushes or removing a high riser blocked with rust (causing the engine to overheat,) are two examples. Both jobs would have been easier on shore, but that's not where boat problems occur. Having tools and being able to correct issues sure beats waiting for a tow and the bill that goes with it. Preventive maintenance certainly makes a boat more reliable, but if you spend a lot of time offshore, consider obtaining towing insurance. It is costly, but certainly worth the expense. Hopefully, you never have to use the service. But one tow bill more then pays for several years of premiums.

Stowage space onboard is always at a premium, but do not cast off without basic tools, electrical tape and (learned from experience) extra: spark plugs, fuel lines, water separators, engine belts and a spare prop. Also, do not forget an extra washer and nut for the prop in case the ones removed are dropped in 30 fathoms of water. The tool box needs to contain a large pair of side cutters capable of cutting a shiny Mustad forged 9/0 stainless steel hook. You know... the kind of hook that's capable of going all the way through someone's hand. Again, first-hand knowledge (no pun intended). A mask and snorkel come in very handy when the need arises to swim under the boat to cut away rope that has entangled the prop and strut. This, I can assure you, will happen on more then one occasion offshore.

Everyone needs to know how to handle the fishing gear and their responsibility once a fish is hooked up. Sharp, pointy, or other potentially dangerous items should be stored immediately after use. Never, ever, place a knife on a seat, for example. Confusion during the excitement of landing fish can get someone hooked, cut, or as the scar on my leg clearly demonstrates, gaffed. I am not the only fisherman this has happened to, it appears to be a common occurrence. Speaking of legs, do not start the day off on the wrong foot. Take it from my derriere and shins, if you trailer a boat, be careful when launching (or pulling the boat out) because those ramps are slippery at low tide.

Throwing a large, still "green" (energetic) fish on the deck is asking for trouble. When this occurs, use caution moving the fish to the kill box. Even species such as tuna need to be treated with respect. The slapping tail of a 100-pound bluefin put my wrist in a brace for most of a summer. It is what I get for trying to grab the tuna's tail by hand instead of with a hand gaff.

One of my favorite movie lines sum up fishermen nicely, "stupid is as stupid does." And I know this sounds stupid, but... live mako belong in the water! Trust me on this one, from experience learned on more then one occasion (I say "experience," my wife says "slow learner"). Sharks do not belong in the boat. It is a little unnerving when gas is squirting from a fuel line onto the deck while a mako takes a tour of your cockpit, sampling the buffet. Apparently a captain's authority diminishes at times like this if he is standing on top of a helm seat shouting orders. Trying to coax the crew out from behind a closed and locked cabin door for assistance apparently falls on deaf ears. You may resolve to tackle the beast yourself, as I did. Have you ever tried to stand on a fiberglass deck coated with gas and oil? Suffice it to say, no one was injured but my wife believes to this day that mako steaks have a strange kind of petroleum favor. I can add that repairing chewed cushions, broken cooler hinges, cracked fiberglass and teeth marks in a gelcoat takes up exactly one summer weekend of precious fishing time. The danger of sharks should be evident, but also be mindful of the sharp teeth of bluefish, kings, and wahoo.

Survival in an offshore emergency may depend on communication. The cost of VHF radios has come down to the point where carrying an extra one should be considered. Do not forget to have an assortment of extra fuses onboard and carry spare batteries for handheld VHFs. Marine VHF radio transmissions are line-of-sight. The curvature of the earth prevents VHF signals from reaching land when far offshore. Depending on antenna height, 30 miles may be about the limit. If your boat's VHF is unable to reach shore from areas you plan to fish, consider adding a SSB (single side band) radio or investing in a Satellite cell phone. SSB radio transmissions can reach shore-based receivers from offshore by "skipping" off the ionosphere and returning to earth beyond the horizon. Satellite phones, depending on the server, have a working offshore range of around 200 miles.

Another life-saving device worth considering is an emergency position indicating radio beacon (EPIRB). Setting off an EPIRB will initiate a wide-scale search that could save you and your crew's lives. Class A, Class B, and Class C operate on VHF frequencies, with Class C being a short range signal. Category 1 and 2 EPIRBs transmit on a dedicated emergency frequency, 406 MHz, which is monitored by satellites and if registered with NOAA, the signal from these 406 MHz EPIRBs can also provide rescue crews with vessel information.

Check the marine forecast before leaving the dock and throughout the day. Be sure fuel is topped off before every offshore trip. Tanks cannot hold too much fuel when fighting the wind and waves of an unexpected storm. Trying to make headway for hours on end burns many gallons.

When the sun and water of Mother Nature combine, she has the upper hand. Protection from the elements is essential for enjoyment while fishing. Sunburn or sunstroke are possibilities if proper care is not taken. Worst yet, is the possibility of skin cancer or eye damage from the combined reflection of the sun coming off the water and direct rays. Chances of sunstroke may be reduced by staying hydrated and drinking plenty of fluids, preferably water. Skin can be protected with long sleeve shirts and pants. Of course, this option is not looked upon favorably when the temperature closes in on triple digits, which is why suntan lotions were introduced. Ingredients in sun screen products protect the skin by blocking harmful UV radiation. The sun protection factor (SPF) is a rating given to the different sun products and refers to how long a person may be in the sun before burning. Everybody's skin is different concerning how long they may be in the sun before being affected. If you can stay in the sun for 10 minutes without burning, a suntan lotion with a SPF of 15 means you may extend your stay in the sun for 150 minutes. Your 10 minutes, multiplied by the SPF factor of 15. The higher the SPF rating the longer a person may stay in the sun before burning. Apply sun protection products often and liberally.

Eye damage called photokeratitis is irreversible sunburn of the cornea that often results in temporary loss of vision. The good news is that it can be prevented by wearing a good pair of polarized sunglasses. Besides being indispensable for observing fish beneath the surface by cutting through the surface glare, quality sunglasses offer eye protection from the dangerous effects of the sun. I use JKruz polarized sunglasses with blue mirrored lenses. The bottom of the ocean has a lot of structure from all the sunglasses which have been accumulated over the years. However, I am not contributing any more. JKruz sunglasses float. Getting hit along side of the head by gaff handles or rod tips which resulted in watching my sunglasses sink to the bottom is a thing of the past. In addition, these glasses have the best clarity of any sunglasses I have used, bar none. This is due to 16 layers of titanium dioxide/silicone used for the mirrored coating, which creates a crystal clear lens. Although they may not have name recognition, I believe they are the finest sunglasses made for fishing. They are available online at www.jkruzinc.com. We've covered the safety issues—now on to rigging the boat.

OUTRIGGERS

If your boat is not equipped with outriggers, serious thought should be given to installing a pair. Although indispensable for spreading out trolling lines and skipping baits when trolling offshore, do not discount their usage when anchored or drift fishing, too. Does it pay to buy top of the line? Do you really get more for you money? As fishermen, many times we make due with what we have because it works or gets us by. A 20' center console can be outfitted with a set of outriggers anywhere from a couple hundred up to a couple thousand dollars. Rig out a serious sportfisherman and your cost is measured in thousands. The decision when outfitting or retrofitting your boat mainly is based upon your wallet's thickness. One important point to consider when selecting a pair of riggers, is that stiff ones perform better than flimsy whippy types. Outriggers equipped with spreaders, which stiffen the poles, are the optimum setup. No spreaders on your riggers? Kits are available to upgrade. Stiff riggers allow double or triple lanyards to be installed, increasing the number of lines that may be pulled off each rigger. Regardless of the type of outriggers on your boat, use a quality outrigger release clip. Success with outriggers hinges on the clip's ability to perform. This small piece of equipment does more then just hold the line. It is the workhorse of the rigger system. There are many release choices hanging on the racks in tackle shops.

My first set of riggers utilized inexpensive clothespin-type clips. Years ago, they were the standard release option for outriggers. Although they did not perform very well when trolling in rough water or pulling medium to large rigged baits or any bait that created a lot of drag for that matter, I made them work by modifying the clip. A rubber band wrapped around the clip increased tension and prevented the line from snapping out. The rubber band trick worked, but, it created flat spots on the fishing lines which left a question about the strength, thus, fishing line was changed more often. The clips worked great if used to suspend bait at a certain depth when anchored or drift fishing. However, for trolling bluewater, which was the main reason the outriggers were installed, the clips left a lot to be desired. Technology now gives us a large selection of release clips. I cannot think of a reason where the clothespin type clips should be considered for use today. Still, I know a couple old timers who swear by them.

Adjustable tension release clips, like the Aftco Goldfinger, provide a decent release for about $15 to $20 a pair. Compare these to the clothespin type clip and the difference is like comparing a canoe to a power boat. The tension adjustment allows for quick changes when switching back and forth from light to heavy baits during a day of offshore trolling. The adjustment can be set allowing just enough tension to hold a bait firmly without tripping from wave action. For marlin fishing, the clip can be set tight enough to prevent the line from popping out of the rigger from non-aggressive bill attacks. The clip also allows a bait to be dropped back or pulled away to excite a marlin that is only taking a look while deciding whether or not to have dinner. This subject is covered in more detail under chapter 10.

When drifting and chunking for tuna, the clip can be used to suspend a bait. A few wraps of the fishing line around the wire before snapping it shut keeps the line from slipping. This trick is handy when you want to provide movement to a diamond jig from wave action while drifting or anchored.

For a few bucks more you can go first class and install roller type clips. As the saying goes, "you get what you pay for." The roller release is extremely smooth when adjusting lines already set. Tension adjustment is very precise and changes can be made in minute amounts. Roller clips, such as the Aftco roller, run around $50 a pair. The releases only have one drawback, they do not allow a line to be held in a fixed position. Regardless of the type of clip used, tension adjustment is crucial for the safety of your outriggers. Do not over-tighten releases, use only sufficient tension to stop the line from popping or necessary for the type of fishing at the time. I snapped a 16' aluminum rigger when a tuna decided to crash a bait. The clip, tightened down way too far, refused to release. A person might believe the fishing line would have broken first but that was not the case. If you find yourself needing a lot of tension, as when trolling a large heavy chrome jet-head lure (some can weigh more than two pounds) for blue marlin, use a #64 rubber band to attach the line to the outrigger release. Rubber bands are capable of holding a surprising amount of weight, but will break long before your rigger is damaged. They also act as a shock absorber when in rough water and prevent lines from snapping out. Their use is ideal when it is difficult to set the correct amount of tension on a release under a lot of stress.

FLAT LINES

The purpose of a flat line clip is to keep the bait down in the water when trolled in the white wash behind the boat. Depending on the width of your transom, anywhere from two to four flat lines may be trolled in this position. Anglers are normally limited by the number of rod holders. However, if your boat is equipped with more then two rod holders for flat lines, consider carrying a pair of suction-cup flat line clips for those days when you want an extra line or two in the white water. Check out Deep Blue Quick Clips for flat lines. The units utilize three suction cups to secure a release clip on the transom of the boat. No more drilling holes through our precious fiberglass or holes in the beautifully finished transom! The unit easily allows for the release to be moved up or down on the transom to match water conditions and keep baits in the proper position. They also provide a clip attached to a lanyard to prevent being lost at sea, just in case the suction cups come loose, and are more then reasonable at around $40 a pair.

GAFFS AND TAIL ROPES

Bringing a fish to the side of a boat is often the easy part. How to get a 200-pound tuna in the boat or what to do with a 300-pound mako with a very bad disposition depends on equipment beside the rod and reel. The amount of money spent to fish offshore can be staggering when taking into account the boat, motor, rods and tackle. However, I am going to recommend you fork out a little more green so you are prepared when that fish of a lifetime is hooked. A large percentage of fish loss occurs at the transom or side of the boat during the gaffing process. User error can be a problem, but the main culprit is not having the proper equipment onboard. The first time I experienced not having the proper equipment was when I hooked into a "real" shark, not the smaller varieties I was used to catching. The topic of conversation during the first hour of the battle was "what the hell is on the end of the line?" The excitement of these moments cannot be put into words. It is the driving force behind bluewater anglers heading offshore. The second hour brought a monster thresher shark into view. A very close view. The 500-pounder decided to surface and swim nonchalantly behind the transom, where 13' of shark well exceeded the transom width. It was at this point that my father-in-law, with a six-foot gaff in hand, looked me in the eye as a smile broke across his face and said, "now what do we do?" At the time, this was the largest fish ever hooked on my boat. I desperately wanted to bring it to the scale. However, without a proper gaff it was not a possibility, which meant... no fish! The 50 class International performed flawlessly, but to this day I still wish I had bought a flying gaff. Moral of the story: have the proper equipment onboard, which includes carrying the proper gaffs.

How many? The answer varies depending on the species you target and the size of your boat. I recommend four. A hand gaff is ideal for moving fish around on-deck and offloading fish at the dock. A straight six-foot gaff (eight if you have high freeboard) with a three-inch hook works well on thinner fish such as dolphin or kings. A straight six to eight foot with a four inch-head handles most tuna or wahoo. A flying gaff with a five- or eight-inch head is mandatory for shark fishing or to land a very large pelagic.

Gaffing fish can be dangerous and caution must be observed. Many smaller gaffs come with a lanyard. Never attach a gaff to your wrist or person—the reason needs no explanation! To avoid losing your balance, brace your legs solidly against the gunwale. Do not reach out for a fish. Be patient and wait until it comes within gaffing range. This is worth repeating: do not be in a hurry nor reach out for the fish. Try to gaff the fish in the front third. Eventually once experience is gained, head shots become routine, reducing the amount of meat ruined from the gaffing process. Regardless of where the fish is gaffed, remember that a successful gaff is one where the fish is in the boat. However, avoid the tail at all cost; tail-gaffed fish are extremely difficult to hold and have accounted for more then one lost gaff on my boats.

Gaff by coming up from underneath the fish whenever possible, which lifts the fish out of the water. Once the tail of a fish is removed from the water chances of escape are reduced. Coming down on top of the fish when gaffing presents the problem of turning the gaff around in the hand so the fish may be lifted, thus giving a chance for escape.

Many anglers use wind-on leaders to ease the task of bringing fish to the boat. I, for one, only use wind-on leaders where I do not intend to change the lure or rig each time offshore. Many wind-on rigs use no more than five- or six-foot leaders. I do not care to have a swivel that close to the bait when trolling. We'll discuss more on this later in the rigging section.

Another option is to use a longer leader and "wire" (pull the fish the final few feet) by hand. Up until several years ago, this was the only way offshore anglers rigged and still today, at least half practice this method. But several deaths have been associated with wiring large fish.

Never, ever take more then one wrap around the hand when wiring a large fish and chance the line binding or tangling around your glove. If you allow the leader to tangle around your hand, once your feet leave the deck, it's the fish that will decide what depth you reach! Speaking of gloves,

The author wiring a blue marlin. Never take a double wrap around the hand when wiring a fish of this size!

a quality pair is essential to prevent the line from cutting into the hand.

Also remember that the leader being taken in should not be underfoot where it can be damaged by being stepped on or worse, become tangled around the feet. Use a five gallon bucket to collect the leader, or allow it to trail in the water behind the boat as it is taken in.

A tail rope is used in conjunction with the gaff for large fish. Normally associated with shark fishing, the tail rope secures the fish to the boat and prevents escape. Tail ropes for shark need to be made with wire to prevent being bitten through. In addition to a tail rope, if your boat is equipped with a tower you may want to consider carrying a block and tackle to ease the process of getting large fish over the gunwale—250-pound tuna can put a hurting on the lower back when being lifted over the side of the boat.

REELS AND RODS

An angler only needs to spend a little time around the docks and gaze at the hardware in the rod holders of charter boats to find out which manufacturers produce equipment that can handle the day to day punishment of offshore fishing. Penn International reels are the gold standard by which others generally are compared. Does this mean other reels on the market are inferior? No, however for the money spent, these reels take abuse and provide years of service with a reasonable amount of care. Tiagra, Daiwa, Alutecnos, and Shimano all manufacture quality offshore trolling reels. Daiwa has an exceptionally smooth drag system. I had the opportunity to test the Okuma Titus gold series for a charter season and found them to be adequate, although they did require frequent maintenance. The end analysis or deciding factor of which type reel is purchased by most anglers comes down to the price tag.

Offshore fishing requires trolling (conventional style) reels about 95 percent of the time. Spinning outfits have their place when bailing dolphin or in a few other circumstances. Yet, there are those that may argue they can use spinning reels to catch everything that swims. This may be true, but after fishing in the deep for the past few decades, it is a point I do not believe worthy of discussion. Suffice it to say, lever drag trolling reels are best. Single or dual speed? Single speed reels work...period. Two speed reels provide power for cranking when set on the low setting, but I have found more often then not, the drag slips on either setting. I seldom use the low speed power setting. It can be used when an angler wants to move a large tuna or blue marlin. But line retrieval is so slow that it is not practical when actually fighting a fish and trying to keep slack out of the line. It all comes down to preference and what you are willing to spend. It is a nice feature, but if pennies are being counted, I do not feel the option is worth the extra expense.

The first matched set of offshore fishing reels that graced my boat were the Penn Senator series, Models 113 (30 pound) and 114 (50 pound). They worked extremely well for the price paid and did everything asked of them. Of course, it took a couple years to gain experience to learn the amount of drag being applied when a fish stretched out a lot of line. Many fish were lost during this learning period since the reels are equipped with star drags. Drags were set with a scale, but with 300 yards of line stretched out, the amount of pressure being applied is affected by drag created from line in the water and ever-changing spool diameter. The star drag system was difficult to adjust during a battle until understanding the "feel" of how much tension was being exerted by the fish. Many anglers believe the drag should be set and left alone. I do not allow clients to adjust the drags on our charter boat, since they are not used to the rods and find it difficult to tell the approximate amount of drag being exerted.

Standard reel sizes for offshore fishing are 30, 50 and 80 class outfits. Seldom, unless pursuing blue marlin or trophy sharks on a regular basis, are 130 class outfits used. If just getting started in offshore fishing and trying to decide what to purchase, stick with 50 class outfits, since they can handle just about any fish hooked up.

If given a purchase choice from today's reel market, I recommend three manufacturers: Shimano Tiagras, Shimano TLD 50s and Penn Internationals. All three exceed my expectations. The Penn Internationals have performed flawlessly for many years. However, I rate the drag system on the Shimano's higher. All these reels have handled everything nature dishes out. They are quality made and certainly up to the task of handling whatever confronts them offshore. However, if spending a few thousand dollars for outfits creates a tightening in the seat of your pants—or worst yet in your wife's—consider the following. I have used Shimano TLD 25 reels and they perform well considering the price. They are not in a class as the previous mentioned reels, nonetheless they are capable of catching fish offshore. This reel is capable of handling 30 class requirements and may be spooled with 50-pound line in a pinch. If an angler shops around, the reel can be purchased without spending a fortune, for around $150. For anglers getting started in offshore fishing, the reels are capable of performing the required task and are a decent investment. Note: do not purchase trolling reels without lever drags. Lever drags allow drag adjustment between the strike and fighting position. Star drag systems are difficult to use for the much-needed option of adjusting the drag during a battle. In case you are wondering if the level wind reels you use in the bay will suffice offshore, the answer is probably no. Blistering runs up to 60-mph tears them apart.

Since I do not want to add another chapter to this book just to discuss the different aspects of spinning reels available for purchase, let's make this simple. The reels should be resistant to salt, equipped with several ball bearings and have a smooth drag system capable of handling at least 20-pound test line. I use Shimano Baitrunner reels because they work. Chances are you have spinning equipment that is used in bay fishing situations that can be converted for use offshore. Unless you plan to do battle with large pelagic such as marlin or tuna on spinning tackle, most saltwater spinning outfits are adequate for catching the different types of fish that we will address where spinning tackle is advised.

If you think the decision of which reel to purchase is tough, the selection of rods only complicates the issue. Many reel manufacturers also make rods and offer packages, matching the correct rod to the reel. For the most part, offshore rods can be grouped into two categories: trolling and stand-up. If you are limited on the number of outfits that can be purchased, select stand-up rods. They can be used in all types of offshore fishing, whether trolling and fighting fish out of a chair or standing up using a belt and harness. Trolling rods, on the other hand, are longer and stiffer, designed to be used only in a chair situation. Leverage does not allow a long stiff rod to be used in stand-up situations. An example would be when chunking for tuna. Coming to your feet to work a tuna to the boat with a stiff six-foot six-inch trolling rod is next to impossible for any amount of time. The lower back gives out due to the pressure created from leverage; all the pressure is against the tip of the rod, which does not bend. It's like trying to hold an eight-foot two-by-four straight out in front of you with five pounds of weight attached to the end. A stand-up rod, however, allows the angler to stand in a more relaxed mode. The butt end of the rod is stiff, but the mid-section and tip of the rod bend sufficiently to transfer the pressure down to the butt of the rod and into the belt being worn by the angler.

SETTING THE DRAG

Next to actually hooking a fish, there is nothing as important in fishing as a drag system that works properly. Care and lubrication of the disc washers keeps the system in pristine condition, smooth, and ready for battle. In addition, the drag needs to be set correctly. Rule of thumb is to set the drag at 20 to 25 percent of the line's breaking strength at a straight pull. Straight pull means the line is pulled off the reel with no bend in the rod. By pulling a scale tied to the end of the line, the drag is adjusted until the proper tension is obtained. The reasoning behind the 25-percent setting is that drag tension increases from line friction created against the rod guides once the line is under pressure and the rod raised to fighting position. Also, the more line taken off the reel, the smaller the spool becomes—which increases the effective drag setting. The line in the water also creates additional pressure. The 25-percent setting provides a safe zone. Now, if an angler is experienced and knows the "feel" of the rod, meaning the angler has a good grasp on how much pressure is on the line, that angler may opt to increase the percentage of drag. How much? It certainly depends on the level of experience, but 35 to 40 percent is not out of the question. However, it must be remembered if this is done, that when in battle, as pressure increases from the fish the angler must lower the rod tip to reduce it.

Many anglers believe a thumb is part of the drag system. It is not!

Increase the drag by using the lever, not by using a thumb on the spool. Experienced anglers may be able to get away with this move by knowing the feel of how much pressure is being applied, but it is a recipe for disaster during the heat of a battle.

TYPE OF LINE

If you ask half a dozen anglers what type of line they prefer, you'll receive seven different answers. Monofilament line is not the only choice, although 99 percent of all offshore reels are spooled with it. There are other options. Fluorocarbon has been used for leaders the past several years. Now, several companies manufacture fishing line made of 100-percent fluorocarbon. I know of no one using it, and it is very expensive. Then there are copolymer lines, which have a nylon mono center coated with fluorocarbon. This makes the line more supple than 100-percent fluorocarbon. In addition, it is less expensive and can be used as a leader in a pinch. I recommend spooling with a quality monofilament.

Remember that when spooling line, you need to do so under pressure. If the line is not spooled tightly, pressure from a fish is capable of making the line cut down into the spooled line, thus causing line separation. When filling reels, place the spool of line in a bucket of water. Use a wet towel on top of the spool to control the amount of pressure necessary to wrap the line tightly on the reel.

Picking out line to spool is like watching your wife pick out a pair of shoes to match her dress. It is not easy. But, before grabbing any spool of line off the tackle shop shelf, decide how serious you are about being in the record books. Very few anglers venture offshore with the intention of breaking a current world record. However, you may want to consider that when fishing blue water, you are in the vicinity of a possible record fish at all times. If this seems important, be prepared and spool reels with a line that is certified to test below the line class. If 30-pound line is on the rod but tests at 31 pounds, the line is disqualified from that class and moves up to the 50 class division—where the fish may not qualify.

For most of us, the only time the thought of catching a record fish crosses our minds is after it is in the boat. But by purchasing a quality line, such as Ande Tournament Monofilament, in case you are lucky enough to catch a scale-tipping fish, the line will qualify for records.

I.G.F.A. RECORDS

This is a brief explanation concerning the International Angling Rules for the International Game Fish Association (IGFA). This is included to give you an idea of what is required or necessary when it comes to setting a record. If serious about being in the record books, it is recommended that you read the complete rules concerning submissions.

The following angling rules have been formulated by the IGFA to promote ethical and sporting angling practices, to establish uniform regulations for the compilation of world game fish records, and to provide basic angling guidelines for use in fishing tournaments and any other group angling activities. The word "angling" is defined as catching or attempting to catch fish with a rod, reel, line, and hook as outlined in the international angling rules. There are some aspects of angling that cannot always be controlled through rule making. Angling regulations cannot insure an outstanding performance from each fish, and world records cannot indicate the amount of difficulty in catching the fish. Captures in which the fish has not fought or has not had a chance to fight do not reflect credit on the fisherman, and only the angler can properly evaluate the degree of achievement in establishing the record. Only fish caught in accordance with IGFA international angling rules, and within the intent of these rules, are considered for world records on the following class of lines:

Metric	U.S. Customary
1 kg	2 lb
2 kg	4 lb
3 kg	6 lb
4 kg	8 lb
6 kg	12 lb
8 kg	16 lb
10 kg	20 lb
15 kg	30 lb
24 kg	50 lb
37 kg	80 lb
60 kg	130 lb

To qualify a catch, a line sample must be submitted in the following fashion with a completed application: Accompanied along with the entire leader, the double line and at least 50' (15.24 meters) of the single line closest to the double line, leader or hook. All line samples and the leader (if one is used) must be submitted in one piece. If a lure is used with the leader, the leader should be cut at the eye attachment to the lure.

Each line sample must be in one piece. It must be submitted in a manner that it can be easily unwound without damage to the line. The recommended method is to take a rectangular piece of stiff cardboard and cut notches in two opposite ends. Secure one end of the line to the cardboard and wind the line around the cardboard through the notched areas. Secure the other end, and write your name and the specified strength of the line on the cardboard. Any line sample submitted that is tangled or cannot be easily unwound will not be accepted.

In addition to the line submission requirements, the following is required concerning photographs: Photographs showing the full length of the fish, the rod and reel used to make the catch, and the scale used to weigh the fish must accompany each record application. A photograph of the angler with the fish is also required. For species identification, the clearest possible photos should be submitted. This is especially important in the cases of hybrids and fish that may be confused with similar species. Shark applications should include a photograph of the shark's teeth, and of the head and back taken from above in addition to the photographs taken from the side. Whether the shark has or does not have a ridge between the dorsal fins should be clearly evident in this photograph. In all cases, photographs should be taken of the fish in a hanging position and also lying on a flat surface on its side. The fish should be broadside to the camera and no part of the fish should be obscured. The fins must be fully extended and not obscured with the hands, and the jaw or bill clearly shown. Avoid obscuring the keels of sharks and tuna with a tail rope. When photographing a fish lying on its side, the surface beneath the fish should be smooth and a ruler or marked tape placed beside the fish if possible. Photographs from various angles are most helpful. An additional photograph of the fish on the scale with actual weight visible helps to expedite the application. Photos taken by daylight with a reproducible-type negative film are highly recommended if at all possible.

The rules regulating leaders, number of hooks, etc. are numerous. Anglers seriously wanting to pursue a record fish who need to familiarize themselves with all the rules may do so at the IFGA website www.igfa.org/index.asp.

EQUIPMENT CARE

At the end of a long day offshore, the first and most important items on my list that need attention are the reels. I have a substantial investment in the line-gatherers and have no choice but to take care of them. Replacement is not an option since my wife controls our checkbook. Nonetheless, regardless of the cost factor, all reels need to be cleaned. A soft mitt with soap and water removes the salt, followed with a light rinse and dry. This assures years of use. Even with constant care after each outing, the end of the fishing season requires maintenance. Begin by removing the reels from the rods and strip all the line off. Corrosion-causing salt finds its way into every nook and cranny and must be cleaned off. A stiff toothbrush with soap and water is ideal for this job. Clean the exterior of the reels thoroughly, followed with a light coat of lubrication. I recommend taking apart, lubricating and cleaning the reels each season. Cleaning the reel's exterior before tackling the interior helps keep down contamination from salt and dirt. The disassembly of a reel is easy—it's the reassembly that can cause a problem. Organization is the key to success in this endeavor. If you saved the schematic when purchasing the reel, now is the time to dig it out.

This is not a project to take on when time is limited. I find dismantling one reel an evening while sitting in front of the TV works for me, when Mother Nature is pelting sleet and snow against the window. As each part is disassembled, it is cleaned, lubricated, and then placed on the work space in the order it was dismantled. Special attention should be given to the drag system, which is the heart of any reel. Corrosion or pitting of any drag washer requires replacement. Dismantling a reel for the first time can be a daunting experience. However, after taking apart, inspecting, cleaning, and reassembling a couple reels, it becomes routine. At the very least, if this is your first attempt taking apart and cleaning a reel, don't lose any parts (in case it is necessary to visit the repair shop for the final re-assembly).

Once finished, remember to back off all tension on the drags for storage. Otherwise, they may get indented or pitted through the winter. Wait to respool new line until spring, before their first use. For those who do not feel comfortable in their ability to tear a reel down, many tackle shops perform the procedure for about $50 a reel. However, do not wait until spring and expect the reels to be done in a couple days. It may take weeks to have the work completed during the spring rush.

Rods should also have been washed and dried when removed from the boat. Now it is time to repeat the process, using a toothbrush to remove all the salt from around the line guides. Take apart and lubricate all rollers. Also lubricate the reel seats; white grease works well for this.

The naked eye cannot detect nicks on the rod guides which cause line fray. Borrow (steal) one of your wife's nylon stockings and run it through and around the guides. If the stocking snags or hangs up, replace the guide. Finally, if the rods look a little worse for wear, give them a coat of rod varnish, and store them in an upright position until the fishing season arrives.

— CHAPTER TWO —
TERMINAL TACKLE

Snaps, swivels and crimps are the connections that take abuse day after day. These items may be small but they handle one big job, keeping the line intact with the fish. Their use is pretty straightforward. However, since there are several types for selection, let's take a look at the options.

SNAP SWIVELS

There is one brand name that takes precedent over the rest: Sampo. These swivels are constructed with quality. In all my thousands of hours of trolling I have only encountered one failure of a Sampo Coastlock snap swivel. I have tried less expensive manufactured swivels which ended up being inferior, with several failing. Spend the money and use Sampo ball bearing snap swivels. When the fish of a lifetime tail-walks across the surface of the water, this is one less item you will need to worry about. Day in and day out they perform and last. Three or four years of service is not out of the question. I have retired some only because the finish was totally removed from all the time spent in salt water. If they are washed along with the rest of the equipment at the end of each day, expect several years of service from the investment. During the off season, before storing them away, spray with a light coat of lubricant.

Like most things in life, there are choices to complicate purchases. Concerning colors, the options are silver and black. Which to use? I cannot recall any charter captains ever utilizing silver. There is always the fear of the shiny swivel being thought of as a meal, and attacked.

There are a couple styles to choose from, too. Use the Coastlock style, not the standard interlock. Coastlock have higher test ratings and more importantly, stay locked. Interlock snap swivels have a way of occasionally coming undone. I, nor anyone I'm familiar with, can figure out how this happens. But on occasion when winding in a line, anglers find an interlock snap to come undone. Hi-Catch also produces a quality ball bearing, escape-proof snap swivel. Unique in their construction, they work and are worth the money spent to guarantee a snap does not come undone. Under no circumstances use any type snap swivel that is not ball bearing; these cheap swivels simply don't do the job.

BARREL SWIVELS

Once again, Sampo is in front of the pack. I use these for any in-line leader connections. For example, when running a spoon off a planer, an extra black ball bearing swivel inserted in the middle of the leader all but eliminates twists. The chunking section of this book recommends using barrel swivels. I cannot afford to use Sampo barrel swivels when chunking since so many rigs are broken off by our charter clients. Instead, I use Rosco barrel swivels. However, they are only used one day and discarded. At less then 10 cents apiece it is a viable option.

There are two other swivels anglers may want to consider in their terminal tackle selection. These are the Spro Power Swivel and the Krok stainless steel swivel made by BillFisher. Either can be used for chunking or for wind-on leaders. Leaders are covered under their own section, but one method of making easy wind-ons is by utilizing one of these swivels. They are smaller then standard swivels manufactured by other companies. So small, in fact, that they have no problem going through rod eyes, and thus can be wound directly onto the reel.

Since no one size snap or swivel handles every situation, it may be wise to begin a terminal tackle collection with the purchase of a kit. At some point every item in the kit will be used. Replenish when necessary until it is found which items are used most often. Then purchase in bulk to reduce cost.

CRIMPS AND SLEEVES

Lures or natural bait can be purchased rigged. However, if an angler is really interested in offshore fishing, it is worth the while to purchase all the items and learn to make their own rigs. In addition, there is personal satisfaction that comes from catching fish on tackle you construct. Crimpers, leader material and sleeves are essential items necessary to get started. Expect to pay $30 to $40 for a decent pair of crimp pliers. Do not skimp on this purchase. A high end pair will push the price near a Ben Franklin, but they last a lifetime.

The decision over which manufactured leader to use is a debatable issue, as is leader poundage. Over time, fishermen develop personal preferences depending on the type of rigs constructed and quarry targeted. Billfishermen are a good example. They tend to use leaders such as Momoi's Diamond Hi-Catch Monofilament, which holds up to the abrasion of a billfish. But, the trade off is a stiff leader. If you are just beginning to dabble in making rigs and feel reluctant to sink a small fortune into an array of leaders and sleeves for any type of rigging, start with a coil of 150-pound leader material. This poundage can be used in a pinch to construct just about any type of offshore rig.

Line connections are made with sleeves using crimpers, not knots, in leader this thick. Once again, preference on the type of sleeve to use is up for discussion. I normally go with aluminum sleeves because they resist corrosion (if the salt is washed off after each use,) and last through one season. Jinkai sleeves in size I or H work well with 150-pound leader. Each pack of 50 sleeves sets you back approximately $6. Rigging kits are available from several sources. Offshore Angler (Bass Pro) carries the World Wide Sportsman rigging kit for $69.99 which includes crimps and a decent pair of crimp pliers for those just entering the sport of offshore fishing.

HOOKS

Size and style depends on the rigging requirements for the species being pursued; appropriate hooks are therefore discussed under each section when addressing each fish or rig.

PLIERS

Purchase a decent pair of needle-nose pliers that have side cutters, along with a pouch for attaching to your belt. They are as important to a fisherman as a hammer is to a carpenter. I've given up spending $50 or more on stainless steel pairs only to leave them as bottom structure on the 100 fathom line. There is no "being careful" when you reach over with pliers in hand, to release a marlin. If you fish hard and catch fish, at some point they are going over. I've found Sears Craftsman pliers work great and come with a lifetime guarantee against rusting... although I have never owned a pair long enough to take advantage of returning them rusted!

— CHAPTER THREE —
RIG IT RIGHT!

The crimpers are in hand and waiting to be used, but there are still a few loose ends that need to be covered before we begin crimping sleeves and getting ready to run offshore. Fishing can test an angler's patience and sanity. No one wants to sit on their boat and watch boats around them catch fish without so much as a nibble on their rods. The reasons possible for this depressing situation are too numerous to list. In this chapter we will cover types of leaders, and how to rig lures and bait—to hopefully prevent you from watching fish being caught, instead of catching them.

LEADER MATERIAL

The type of leader plays a major role in success or failure, and seems to be overlooked by many fishermen. Anglers use leaders that are overkill in many situations, which decreases the odds of hooking fish. This occurs in trolling leaders as well as when chunking or casting to fish. Fishermen take care to conceal a hook in bait, then use a leader that looks like rope to fish. Fish eyes and human eyes are not that different. Being a dive master, I have spent many hours at the bottom of the ocean observing fish, as well as on top fishing. Fifty-pound test monofilament line appears as 1/8" rope, to my eyes underwater. The line is magnified by the lens in the mask, nonetheless the line is very visible. One can only imagine how it looks to fish. Fish have good eyesight and shy away from bait and lures on heavy leader when in clear water. Of course, visibility is not the only concern when selecting leaders. A balance must be found between the visibility aspect with leader weight for the species targeted and the ability of fish to bite through the leader. The idea, "I will use the same leaders for what ever might bite" should be discarded. Concentrate on rigging for the intended species. This mistake is often observed when offshore anglers planning to troll head for the canyons, rigged for tuna. Do not rig 400-pound leaders when running offshore for a day of tuna trolling, on the presumption that a blue marlin "might" be raised and hooked. Sure, tuna may be caught on 400-pound test, but bites become far and few between due to the visibility of the leaders. Landing large fish on light leaders is possible. When bluefin exceeding 200 pounds are being caught chunking, there is no need for 100-pound leader, assuming you are using 30- or 50-pound test fishing line. Tuna seldom bite through 50-pound leader. There may be abrasion from the mouth but normally 50-pound leader holds up. Fifty-pound test line is going to break at 50 pounds—leader material in excess of this weight only swings the pendulum in the tuna's advantage by increasing the line's visibility.

Here is the choice: hook-up fish on light leader or watch others hook fish. There are times tuna do not seem affected by heavy leader, such as when fishing in cloudy water or on overcast days. But often, that leader size will make a huge difference. So keep in mind, if you are not hooking up, consider dropping down in leader poundage.

There is a debatable issue whether using monofilament versus fluorocarbon leaders really makes a difference when trolling. It is important to understand the difference between the two choices in order to make an educated decision. First, fluorocarbon is made from a chemical called... you guessed it, fluorocarbon. You no doubt have heard that fluorocarbon disappears underwater. This is not exactly correct, but close. Fluorocarbon has nearly the same light refraction rate as water, which explains how it "disappears" once beneath the surface. How does this occur? The refractory index of water has a value of 1.33. If it were possible to manufacture fishing line to this same value, it would be totally invisible in water. Until that is accomplished, fluorocarbon is the closest line available to invisibility with a value of 1.42. In comparison, quality monofilament's value is 1.62. Some braided line rates over 2.0. I have read that our government has a water camouflaging program that has duplicated 1.33. So, invisible line may be in our future. However, until that time, fluorocarbon is the best option for invisible line. Okay, but how important is this difference for a trolling leader? This is where the debate begins. No one would argue the fact that tuna see monofilament leader when used in chunking situations. Tuna can also see fluorocarbon in clear water, but of course trolling is a different animal, with white water, movement and turbulence. Is the extra expense worth it for trolling leaders? Yes, if you can find a few more bucks in your wallet. The use of fluorocarbon can only improve your odds of hookups. Is fluorocarbon absolutely necessary? No, but why not increase the odds of catching fish? In the big scheme of offshore fishing expenses, the additional cost for fluorocarbon is not extreme. In addition, there are other benefits to using it over mono as leaders.

Fluorocarbon is imperious to ultraviolet radiation, meaning it does not deteriorate when exposed to sunlight, as monofilament does. The worry of buying in bulk with a shelf life if exposed to UV light is of no concern. On the other hand, anglers need note, mono takes hundreds of years to breakdown and dissolve; fluorocarbon may take thousands, and scientist really do not know for sure. Anglers need to take precautions and protect the environment, and of course, never discard mono or fluorocarbon line in the water.

What other benefits are derived from using fluorocarbon over mono? How about being more abrasion-resistant? Or the fact that the outer skin of the line does not allow water to penetrate? Mono lines soak up to 10 percent of their weight in water, while fluorocarbon soaks up zero to three percent. Monofilament knots swell and become tight due to absorbing water, but this does not occur with fluorocarbon, meaning the fluorocarbon knot must be tied more exactly. If so, it is as strong, if not stronger then, knots tied in mono. As with mono knots, lubricate the line by wetting to make sure the knot snugs down tight.

For years I used single-strand wire trolling leader and was slow warming up to the idea of monofilament leaders. Wire is absolutely necessary when rigging for wahoo or other toothy critters. There are times I still use wire leaders in place of monofilament when fish are finicky, but with the invention of fluorocarbon, wire has fallen by the wayside in my use. Nonetheless, there is still a place offshore for wire leaders and it can be used with great success. Wire is a cheap alternative to fluorocarbon. Two choices confront anglers selecting wire leader. Single-strand or multi-strand. I like single-strand stainless steel, such as Malin, in coffee color. The thin diameter all but disappears in the water. It is ideal when rigging natural bait such as Ballyhoo since it has its own pin to hold the bait; more on this later. There are two downfalls with single-strand wire: it is difficult wiring fish with the thin diameter, and once the leader kinks it is finished. The kinking normally occurs when wiring fish. Once kinked it must be discarded—do not use wire with a kink, it all but guarantees line separation.

Multi-strand wire comes made with seven individual strands or 49 strands rolled into one wire line. The advantage over single-strand is the flexibility. The 49 strand is extremely flexible. Both are effective for toothy adversaries with the exception of sharks. When in an extended battle with large sharks, the teeth are capable of cutting the individual strands one at a time until the leader fails. Shark leaders and rigs are covered in detail under the shark section, since this is a specialty type of fishing.

I recommend keeping the length of trolling leaders somewhere between 12' and 15'. Longer leaders certainly do not hurt chances of success, but increase the possibility of tangles occurring as the leader is gathered when wiring fish. If you are concerned about catching a possible record fish, remember that the leader and double line may not exceed 30' in total length. An offshore loop is normally installed on the end of leaders for attachment to the line's snap swivel.

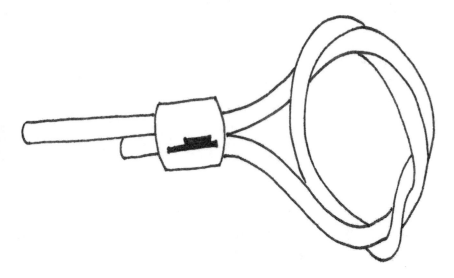

An offshore loop: Slide crimp onto leader. Loop line, come back through loop and into crimp.

DOUBLE LINES AND KNOTS

A double line is exactly what the name implies, two lines combined from the main fishing line to which a snap swivel is usually tied. Double lines typically use a knot called a Bimini Twist to secure the line together. This knot is sometimes referred to as a 20-twist knot. It is an excellent knot but awkward to tie. It takes anglers proficient at tying the knot a couple minutes to complete. It is a great knot and worth your time to learn and practice. However, since we want to get on the water and fish, in place of a Bimini, I am going to suggest first learning a knot I refer to as a Hillbilly Bimini, or commonly know as a Spider Hitch. It is very quick to tie and almost as strong as a Bimini. When in a hurry or if you find yourself constantly changing and cutting lines when fishing, it is the way to go for fast re-rigs. I tie this knot making the double line about 12' in length. Combined with a 15' leader I am well under the 30' limit for IGFA qualification.

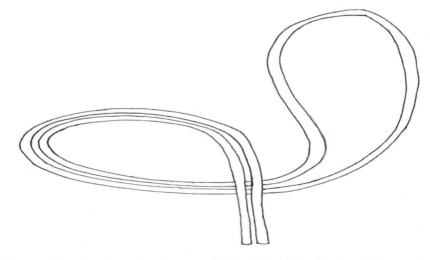

Determine the length of your desired double leader. Place a loop just above that point.

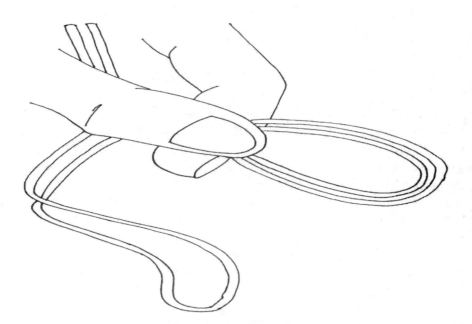

Hold the loop between your thumb and forefinger.

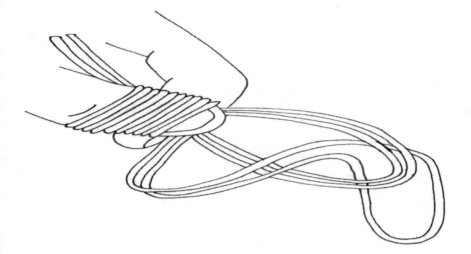

Wrap the leader six to eight times around your thumb. While holding the loop between your thumb and forefinger, gently pull on the
double line so the loops come off your thumb one at a time.

Lubricate the knot well and apply tension to all four strands equally,
until the knot is snug.

What is the advantage of a double line? Once a double line is within reach, the person wiring can apply considerable pressure on the fish with a double line in hand until the actual leader is reached. Additionally, as the wraps of the double line are wound onto the reel, the drag may be increased to add pressure. Note, this can be a dangerous move if the double line is pulled back off the reel and the drag is not loosened. At the end of the double line, a Cat's Paw knot is used to secure the swivel to the line.

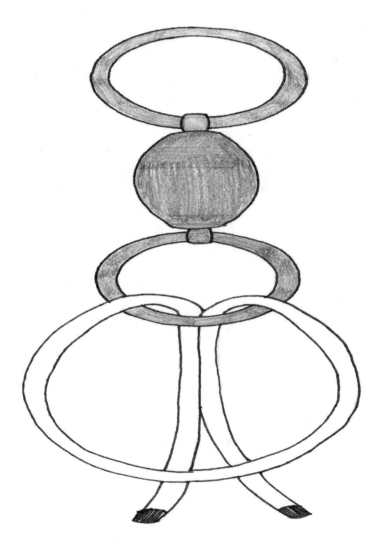

Thread end of the double leader through the swivel.

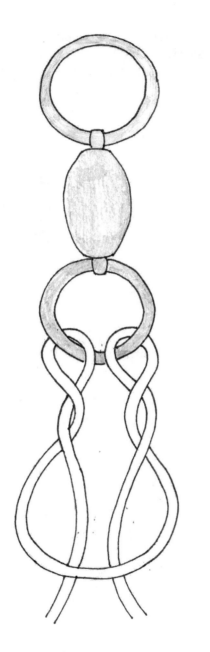 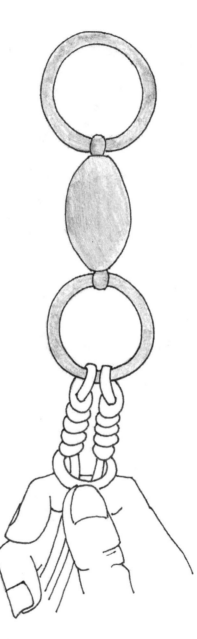

Rotate the swivel through the center of the loops four to six times depending on the thickness and flexibility of the line.

Lubricate thoroughly, and snug up the knot. It may be necessary to use your thumbnail to help snug the knot.

As I mentioned earlier, the Bimini Twist is more difficult to tie then a Spider Hitch. But, for the offshore enthusiast rubbing elbows with those who live and breath the bluewater, it is a knot that must be known!

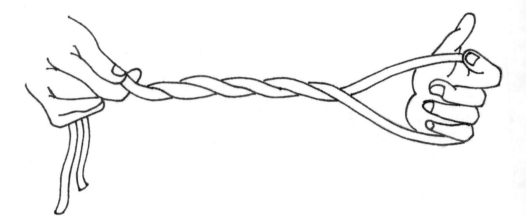

The first step is to twist the line a minimum of 20 times.

This knot is best tied with two people, but anglers experienced at tying the knot can utilize a stationary item, such as a cleat. Tension must be kept on the knot from this point forward.

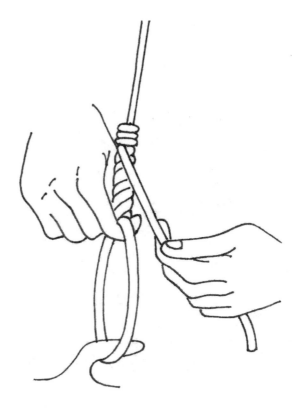

• The length of the double line (loop with finger inserted) can be made to suit your needs. For offshore trolling, I make the length approximately 12', but this length varies depending on application.

• Use your finger and pull up in the loop to snug up the 20-line twist. While increasing pressure with your finger, the knot actually begins to twirl. At this point you slightly release tension on the tag end and the line wraps down overtop the line twist. This is the most difficult part of the knot to master.

• When tying the knot alone, I wrap the double line around my foot and use my knee in place of the finger, snugging up the loop. With a little practice, your foot can apply the tension to twirl the knot, leaving both hands to control the line running down over top the twist.

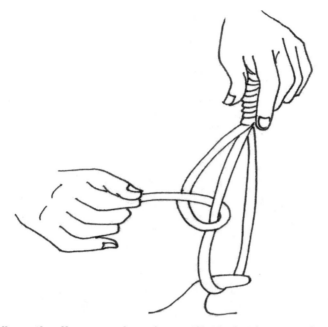

When the line running down the twist is completed, tie a half-hitch to prevent the knot from unraveling.

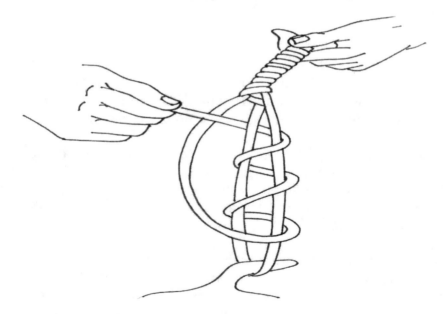

Complete the knot as showed with four or five turns around both lines. Moisten the knot well and pull on the tag end until tight.

When completed correctly, this knot actually acts as a small shock cord. If you apply pressure to the knot you can observe it stretch.

There is one other knot that is often used in conjunction with the Bimini or Spider Hitch. This is the Albright, also known as the Surgeon's knot. The knot also may be used to join two lines of unequal diameter together, such as the main line to a leader when a swivel connection is not desired.

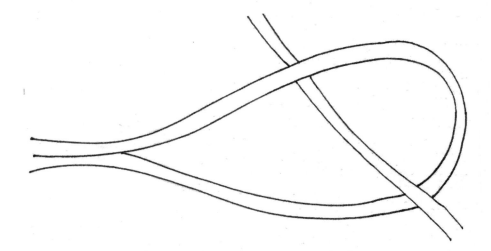

When possible, place the loop in the heavier of the two lines when tying the knot. Begin as shown, running a tag end through the loop.

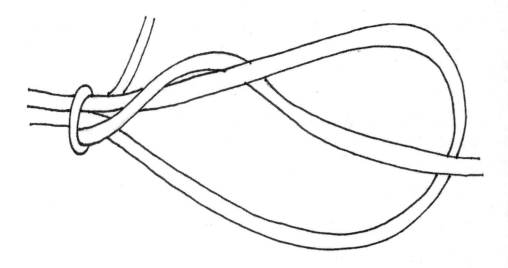

While holding the tag end with your fingers, wrap the line around all the lines 12 to 15 times, working down towards the loop.

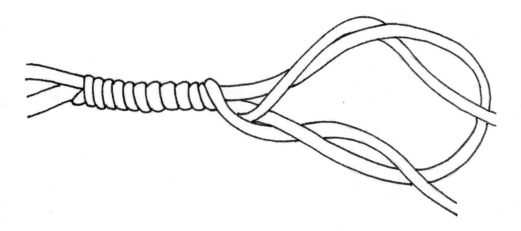

Insert the tag end back through the loop.

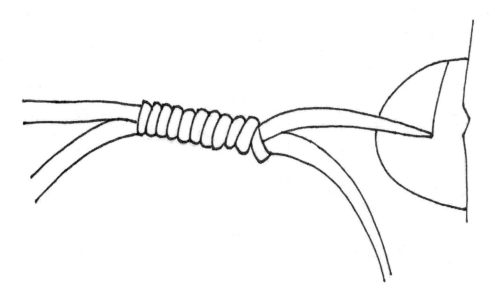

Wet the line. While keeping tension on the tag end, use your thumb nail to work the line down tight over the loop.

Pull both lines to snug the knot, then trim off excess tag line.

One final knot all anglers should know is the Improved Clinch, or "Fisherman's Knot." It's useful for direct line-to-hook or line-to-swivel connections. First, pass the line through the eye of the hook. Take several turns around the main line. Come back through the first line twist. Take the tag end back through the large loop and lubricate well before firmly snugging up the knot.

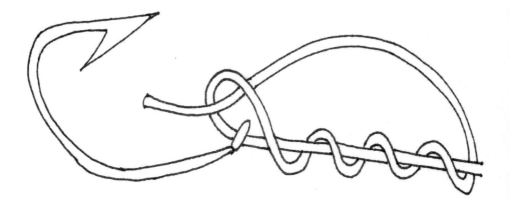

Pass the line through the eye, make four to six turns, then come back through the loop made by the first twist.

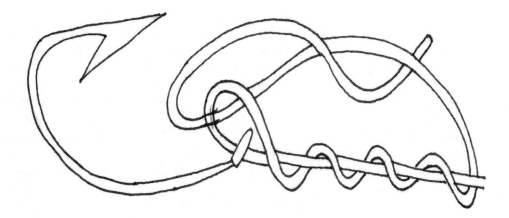

Turn the line back, and put it through the loop you just made with the line.

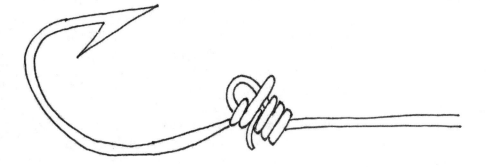

Lubricate the line before snugging up the knot.

WIND-ON LEADERS

Wind-on leaders remove the task of wiring a fish by hand until the gaff can be sunk. They also eliminate having the coils of leader in the cockpit, where they can become a hazard or be damaged underfoot. The original design of wind-on leaders used a piece of heavy Dacron line to form a loop on the end of the leaders. This loop was connected to the loop of the double line. This makes for a snap-less connection, which allows the leader to be wound through the eyes and onto the reel. However, as with all good ideas, there is still a problem as far as I am concerned. A swivel is required to prevent line twist. This normally is inserted about five feet from the bait or lure. In this manner, most of the leader can be wound onto the reel until the last five feet, which places the fish within gaffing range.

I do not feel the trade off is worth it. This places the swivel in close proximity to the bait, which I believe causes leery fish like tuna or sailfish to shy away on occasions. I know many fishermen that would argue this point and use the original wind-on leaders with great success. Nonetheless, I gave up using this type of wind-on several years ago and went back to regular leaders and wiring fish. Until, that is, Spro came out with their line of swivels so small they have no problem going through the rollers or eyes on a rod. At last, a true wind-on leader can be made with no swivel near the bait and where the leader and swivel may be wound all the way onto the reel. In addition, the leaders are easy to construct compared to the original wind-on design, which required threading the mono into the Dacron. I like the Spro 80- or 130-pound test swivel on 30- and 50-class rods, respectively. Spro also manufactures swivels made exclusively for use as wind-ons. These are called Spro Heavy Duty Bullets. They are available in 150-, 240- or 340-pound test all the way up to 2550-pound for commercial use.

Targeting large fish like blue marlin or sharks? No problem rigging 80 or 130 class outfits in the same manner. Catching marlin or sharks with wind-on leader may be vigorously opposed by many professional fishermen. When using heavy tackle, some anglers feel winding a swivel through the rollers or eyes of a rod increases the chance of a snag or hang-up resulting in a broken line. Hand-wiring large fish like shark or blue marlin eliminates this possibility. However, I feel the dangers of wiring a huge fish by hand outweigh the potential disadvantages of using wind-ons. So I use the wind-on system, and believe it is worthwhile for experimentation on your part.

— CHAPTER FOUR —
ARTIFICIAL LURES

The average offshore angler spends just shy of $600 a season on fishing tackle, according to the American Sportfishing Association. This is easy to accomplish with prices of $30 or more for some lures. There are literally thousands of choices in catalogs and hanging on display racks in tackle shops. Do they all catch fish? I guess they all did at one time or another. Which ones should be purchased and pulled in your spread? The decision is based on a combination of the species targeted, imitating available bait, and angler's preference. No wonder anglers can become overwhelmed.

There are basic dependable lures that produce. Some colors are preferred and work well for certain species. Local preferences change as anglers move up and down the Atlantic seaboard. However, certain basic lures have been producing fish for decades. They are dependable and work just about everywhere. With that being said, there is no better indicator of what to pull in your spread for the area you fish then the lures dragged each day behind charter boats. An evening walking around the docks when fish are abundant offshore means captains and mates have smiles on their faces—and information is loose on the lips. Every fisherman likes to talk about what they caught after a successful day offshore. Talking and asking questions on these days can be very productive time spent in gathering information.

COLOR CHOICE

It may be prudent to understand how color has an effect and why it needs to be taken into consideration, before we begin skirting natural bait or picking out those killer lures and securing them to leaders.

"Caught all of them on green, wouldn't touch another color!" Statements like this are heard around the dock all the time. Does color really make a difference? The National Marine Fisheries declares, "Despite the opinion of many sport fishermen, fish can see color shadings, reflected light, shape and movement." Color shadings? Like color is not enough of an issue, now shadings make a difference? Possibly! Take this into consideration: A new technique called microspectrophotometry (MSP) can tell if fish possess the necessary hardware in their eyes to distinguish color, and seems to confirm that fish have cones to detect color and rods to detect light in different species.

Early studies more then 20 years ago showed marlin and tuna to be color blind. Microspectrophotometry is now proving those findings to be incorrect. Of course, they could have saved many dollars by asking seasoned fisherman if color makes a difference.

Fish and human eyes are very similar. Humans have three types of cones. Each cone can detect different wavelengths distinguishing colors of red, green and blue. When put together, the human eye can discern more than 300,000 shades of color. Great, we can see color, but how about fish? Well, catfish have no cones, which means no ability to see color. They do, however, have rods allowing them to distinguish light better then the human eye, necessary when foraging for food on the murky bottom. Different species of fish have different types of cones and rods. It's been found that most predatory fish have cones that should detect color, some possibly with supreme color vision potential. The striped marlin's eye was found to have three cones that may create the ability for color discrimination. More testing needs to be conducted, however, early indications show bigeye tuna, swordfish, yellowfin tuna, and sailfish all have one or more cones capable of sensing some type of wavelength. This does not necessarily indicate that fish have the ability or brain function to process the color information, but it seems odd that nature would provide the eyes with the ability to see color and not provide the brainpower to understand it.

What does this tell us as anglers? For now, at least until more studies are completed, we must assume pelagics have the ability to process color. We'd better use color/depth charts to choose our lure colors, because certain colors are going to be the key when it comes to putting fish in the box.

The decision of color choice is no more evident then when walking up and down isles of a tackle shop trying to pick out those lures we feel will catch fish. Certain species of fish appear to be partial to certain colors. It does not appear to be a random choice on the part of the fish since they consistently pick out the same ones. Since each fish is different, chapter 10 covers which color(s) seem to be preferred by each type of fish, on an individual basis.

One more factor must be considered in the color controversy: the ability of color to be observed in saltwater. Light behaves differently in water then it does in air. Colors of light move at different wavelengths and are absorbed when traveling through water. The longest wavelengths are the first lost. Which means, as depth increases in saltwater with average clarity, colors are lost in this order: Red at 10', orange at 20', yellow at 30', green at 60', blue at 100' and purple at 110'. Exceptionally clear water increases the depth while overcast skies, algae, floating sediment, or lack of sunlight at dawn and dusk reduces the depth. A red drone pulled on a planer at 35' appears as a dull shade of dark color. However, if pulled at five feet, the red color appears as red and could make a difference.

Regardless of color, can artificial lures out-fish trolled natural bait? Yes, there are times they are in a class by themselves and produce unbelievable results. Here's my list of "required" lures for the artificial arsenal. These lures may be bought pre-rigged or you can rig them yourself. My recommendations for self-rigging are included, based on what has proven successful for me. There are additional lures you may want to include in your arsenal when targeting specific species. Many are discussed under each individual species section.

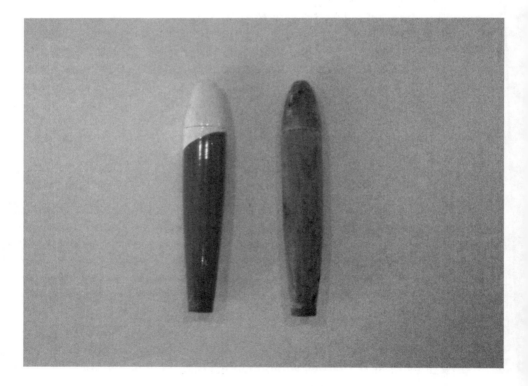

The offshore tackle arsenal is not complete without cedar plugs.

CEDAR PLUGS

The best place to start is always at the beginning, and I know of no offshore lure that has been around longer then the cedar plug. I can find no history on this lure, but have often wondered—who in their right mind would pull a piece of wood as bait? The cedar plug very possibly may have been the first artificial bluewater lure. My educated guess is that many years ago, seafarers, after exhausting their food supply and anything that could be used for bait, needed to come up with something to catch fish for survival. I can picture starving men whittling pieces of wood, attaching hooks and trolling them behind ships. Cedar was used on sailing ships, so it makes sense the lure was made of cedar. I reckon sailors caught fish and fended off starvation. Of course, this is purely conjecture on my part, but I cannot imagine any other reason why a sane person would drag a plain piece of wood to catch fish!

One thing is for sure, anglers have been pulling cedar plugs for many years with success. Best known for catching tuna, they are capable of catching just about everything else that swims in the Atlantic. The only species I have not hooked on a cedar plug is a blue marlin. On the other hand, I do not troll cedar plugs when I am targeting blue marlin, so they have not had the opportunity to swallow one.

The streamline shape resembles a torpedo and gives the appearance that it would have no action in the water—wrong! Once the lure reaches a speed of about six knots it becomes active by darting and dancing through the water, resembling baitfish trying to flee. Once only made of cedar and natural in color, they are now offered in an array of colors, aluminum and plastic. Aluminum models offer the option of interchanging bodies creating many possible color combinations. I do not know any charter skipper that does not carry an array of cedar plugs. They catch fish and should be one of the first lures placed in the tackle chest. The lures may be fished on long riggers, short riggers, or my favorite location, on flat lines close to the boat, where they really produce fish while dancing in and out of the white water.

Cedar plugs are easy to rig. Begin with a 12' leader in 125- to 150-pound test. Many anglers rig cedar plugs on 250-pound test, however, the heavier leader takes away from the lure's movement. Stay to the light side for best results. Crimp a loop at one end then slide the leader through the plug, beginning from the head of the lure. Finish by crimping a needle-eye style 9/0 hook (a standard eye does not fit into the base of the lure,) and slide the hook up into the body of the plug.

Daisy chains can be made from just about any type of lures and the cedar plug is no exception. There are two ways to rig chains with cedar plugs. I normally use three cedar plugs on my daisy chain. The first cedar plug is rigged in standard fashion. Next, insert a crimp approximately 20" up the leader from the last plug to prevent the second cedar plug from sliding down the leader. Then place a crimp 15" above the middle plug and slide the last cedar plug on the leader. This gives the illusion of three bait fish zigging and zagging through the water. The theory between placing 20" between the last Cedar plug and 15" between the first two is that it creates an illusion of a trailing baitfish. In nature, it is survival of the fittest. The sick and weak are the first picked off or eliminated by predators, which is normally the last in line or in our case, the trailing bait. This theory is true when constructing all daisy chain type lures.

A second way to rig cedar plugs is as a drop chain. The last plug is rigged as normal. Take two other plugs and attach each to a six-inch piece of 250-pound test leader. A crimp at the end of each short leader secures the cedar plug. Attach the leader of each plug to the main leader using crimps spaced at 15" and 20". The jumping and dancing of the first two plugs is exaggerated as compared to the standard cedar plug daisy chain.

SPREADER BARS

I am not sure where the idea of spreader bars developed. Probably some angler figured if a daisy chain worked to catch fish, then three or more daisy chains together should raise more fish. They were not wrong! Spreader bars belong in just about every spread. Versatile in that they may be pulled in several positions, they catch fish pulled from just off the transom, to long riggers. Most noted for catching tuna, do not discount their ability to raise and catch white marlin or other species. The typical spreader bar has three or five daisy chains of lures or skirts attached to a bar anywhere from two to four feet in width. One of the most popular type lures or skirts used in making spreader bars are plastic squid. The last squid in the middle string contains the hook, which is the farthest skirt or lure from the spreader bar. Spreader bars are beneficial since they create the appearance of a school of bait splashing on the surface. Predators looking up from the depths at a spreader bar see the school, with a lone baitfish trying to catch back up. This is the appearance anglers should try to achieve when making or selecting a spreader bar. Color and shape of the components used, along with spacing of the individual skirts or lures, plays a roll in the amount of fish caught. However, the main attraction is the surface disturbance, imitating fleeing bait with one bait left behind.

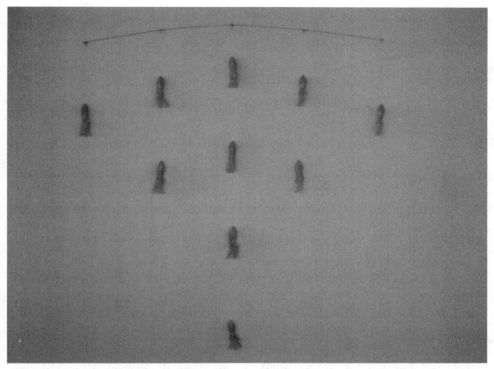

**The last bait slightly trailing the spreader bar's "school" is the one
fish will attack.**

Ideally, a spreader bar should be pulled off of 80 class outfits due to
the amount of drag created, but, 50 class outfits work with smaller versions
of spreader bars. Position in the spread may vary and depending on the
mood of the fish can be productive in each of the following locations:

• Pulled right off the transom, as in eight to 10' behind the boat, it attracts
fish to the bar and to the flat lines positions. I have caught yellowfin on
spreader bars as close as four feet off the transom, but one must remember that vicious attacks on spreader bars so close require a light drag setting to prevent line separation, because with such a small length of line
out there's little to no line to stretch. Smaller bluefin and often schools of
yellowfin are enticed by the spreader bar in this close location. Bigeye also
have no problem taking bars right behind the boat. The bar needs to be
held close to the water which means flatline clips must be used. Set the flat
line clips with just enough pressure to prevent release. Pull the spreader
bar so the bar is actually out of the water and only the squid or lures touch
the water. Locate other flat lines behind and off to the sides of the spreader

bar for additional bites when fish are raised.

• Short riggers work well for pulling the bar, since a flat line bait may be placed in front and off to the side of the bar. Pulled from this position, the long rigger can also be run 20' behind the spreader bar, creating a second illusion of a trailing baitfish. From the short rigger position, adjust the bar so it rides just out of the water.

• A long rigger can be used to pull spreader bars as well, or one can even be pulled from the shotgun position. Many anglers use a spreader bar made with birds attached to the bar, commonly called splash bars. The bird creates additional splash when pulled from these locations since the bar is in the water.

• The bars are also ideal for use as a teaser. Try pulling two spreader bars in place of teasers. This places the bars approximately 25' to 30' off the transom. Using the bars as teasers does not allow for a hook to be used, but this location allows anglers to utilize the short riggers for placing baits directly behind the spreader bar. This permits the use of lighter tackle, since only a lure or bait is pulled off the rod, instead of the entire spreader bar. Place a single bait from the short rigger five or six feet behind the bar. This is a very successful system for using a teaser bar to catch fish. In addition, by using the spreader bar as a teaser, the weight and drag of the bar is eliminated when a fish is hooked-up.

I believe it is impossible to choose an incorrect color for a spreader bar, but if only using one bar, I would go with the multicolored nine or 12" rainbow squid utilizing a 36" five-position bar. Spreader bars do not come cheap when picking one off the shelf, with prices ranging from $50 to $200 or more for fully constructed units. However, making spreader bars is fairly easy and the cost can be cut in half. Light-weight bars can be bought for around $6 apiece at most tackle shops. Anglers who want to further reduce their cost can purchase 3/32" or 1/8" stainless steel welding rods and bend them to make their own bars. When constructing spreader bars, the inexpensive cost allows anglers to make several with different styles and colors of skirts or rubber/plastic squids. Shop around—six-inch rubber skirts can be purchased for as little as $.50 apiece, bringing construction cost under $20 for completed bars.

Many pre-made bars are constructed with overkill, using 250-pound test leader or more. I have found 130-pound leader more then sufficient. I have also found the lighter leader seems to draw more strikes then heavy.

Construction is simple; each lure/skirt is placed on the leader with a float and crimp. If pulling three lines off a bar, use four skirts on the two outside lines and six skirts on the middle line. If using a five position bar, position the skirts or lures as indicated in the photo. These setups work for me; you may want to use more or less skirts when creating your own fish-attraction bars. I have used 19 six-inch squid with 12" spacing between squid creating a spreader bar 10' in length. It is a killer on yellowfin at times. You may want to consider using 15" squid to create an extremely large fish-attraction unit. Construction is only limited by your imagination.

In addition to the previous mentioned locations for pulling a spreader bar, try pulling two bars off the short riggers. Place the bars about 100' to 125' behind the transom. With this spread, make sure you place a rigged bait on a flat line between the two spreader bars. If using two spreader bars as teasers, place a third bar pulled from the shotgun position in the middle of the spread. This covers the transom for close bites and the mid-spread area as well. Do not be afraid to experiment with location of the bars. Many days, a short rigger spreader bar pulled on the fourth wave and a second short rigger bar pulled on the seventh wave on the opposite side raises enough fish to fill the kill box.

Many billfish rise to spreader bars, but, there is no way to drop back the spreader bar to hook the fish. However, I have found that by pulling the bar slightly away from the marlin, a savage attack can sometimes be obtained. Attempt to set the hook when the weight of the marlin is felt.

GREEN MACHINE

This lure is an old stand-by in the northeast. Moving south towards the Carolinas, there is a possibility of being ridiculed for trolling plastics, where pulling "meat" is very popular. But, those that do not fish Green Machines are only cutting themselves short. Anglers fishing the northeast would be chastised if they did not have them onboard, and I would not consider running offshore without several. There are days I have pulled a spread of nothing but Green Machines. They can be that good in producing fish. Seldom do I begin a day of trolling without at least one in the spread. There are four models, the regular 12" plastic head which is the most popular, and also a nine-inch style. There's also a 12" weighted head which runs deeper, and a 12" soft head which billfish find more appeasing to the mouth. The soft head allows an extra second or two to set up on a marlin before it spits the lure. These lures are excellent when used individually, on spreader bars, or my favorite—a daisy chain.

I cannot count the number of tuna that committed suicide by attacking a Green Machine daisy chain. It is by far my favorite lure chain. Construction is simple, utilizing three standard 12" Green Machines. Cut a piece of 150-pound leader material 18' to 20' in length. Begin with the business end of the daisy chain and secure the hook. I like the Mustad #7982HS in size 7/0, a stainless steel double hook. It really puts a sting in the tail of the lure and increases strike to hook-up percentages. Rig in a manner where the hook does not protrude past the end of the skirt. Double loop the leader through the eye of the hook, and crimp on a sleeve. I crimp each sleeve two times. Firm pressure is used with the pliers when crimping. However, do not "crush" the sleeve or use excessive force which can damage the line. Slide on the red beads (which come with the lure) followed by a Green Machine. Now, before going any further, check hook placement. It may be necessary to add or remove beads so the hook does not protrude past the skirt. Once satisfied with the hook's location, slide on another sleeve followed by beads and a second Green Machine. Measure 36" from the end of the first lure and crimp the sleeve as a stop for the second lure. Repeat the process with the third Green Machine. However, this time only measure up approximately 30". Construct this chain to give the earlier discussed illusion of a trailing weak prey. Finally, double-loop and crimp the end of the leader. Place the hook around a solid object (a cleat works well) and pull on the leader to test sleeves for slippage. It does not take long to learn the optimum amount of pressure required to crimp a sleeve.

Anglers can rig the lure and save about 35-percent compared to the cost when purchased already rigged. Plus, when rigged as shown, the lure has better hook-up percentage then single-hooked pre-rigs.

I find the Green Machine daisy chain behind a bird pulled WWB (way, way back) to be deadly. There is also the theory of placing a larger lure in the rear giving the appearance of smaller bait being chased. I put this theory into practice and came up with the following tuna rig.

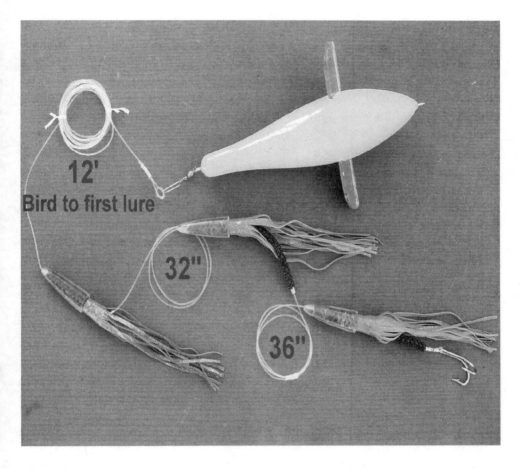

The Green Machine daisy chain/bird rig constantly produces yellow-fin and bluefin tuna in the way, way back position.

DANCING SQUID

My favorite use for a rubber squid is rigged to "dance." This rig is a take-off of the commercial green-stick configuration which is popular in southern waters and used to catch tuna with great success. The photo is self explanatory for the rigging. There is a swivel inserted in the middle of the 250-pound, 40'-long leader. The white squid is clipped onto this swivel when trolled. Rig the nine-inch squid using a Mustad #7982HS 5/0 double hook on 250-pound leader. The hook should be near, but not extend past, the end of the squid. Use a two-ounce sinker and crimp to set the hook at the proper distance. The weight tends to keep the lure from tangling when it jumps out of the water. The two 12" smokers are rigged on 400-pound mono. The stiffness of this line keeps these lures from twisting and tangling. Rig the trailing smoker with a 9/0 hook. Pull the rig off an 80 or 130 class outfit. There are times you will hook up two tuna, one on the squid and one on the smoker. I am not a fan of heavy leader, however, when two 80-pound tuna are trying to tear the rig apart, heavy is necessary. Pull the rig off a rigger unless your flying bridge is very high, in which case you may be able to run the rig in the middle of the spread. It does not produce as

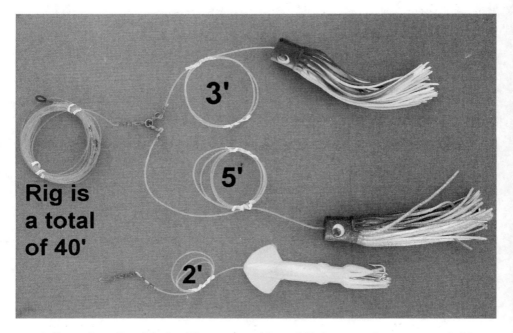

A Dancing Squid rig. The recreational fisherman's green-stick!

well as when run in flat water to the side of the boat, however. Troll the rig so that the two smokers ride on the third or forth wave.

The following is important and must be observed for the rig to produce tuna: the squid should only be in the water 75-percent of the time and must appear to be jumping out of the water (thus the name "Dancing Squid"). Understand, the squid needs to jump off the waves and become airborne. Adjustments to accomplish this are done by either taking in or letting line out, or by changing the length of the squid's leader. The rig imitates the feeding of fish. The two 12-inch smokers dive and splash, while the squid jumps in front trying to flee. Do not be surprised when yellowfin or bluefin tuna go ballistic and clear the water to grab the squid in mid-air.

DAISY CHAINS

Charter boats carry at least a couple squid daisy chains in the tackle locker. The reasoning behind artificial squid in the spread is easy—everything in the ocean eats squid. Do they produce fish everyday? No, but neither do any other baits. However, when the first tuna of the day is thrown on the deck and it spits out squid, the decision of what to pull is pretty easy.

There are two ways I construct this rig. One chain uses two six-inch and one nine-inch Moldcraft squid. The other chain has half a dozen six-inch squid. On any given day, the size of squid being fed upon dictates which chain I pull.

To construct one, crimp a hook to the end of the line. I use a double 7/0 for nine-inch and double 5/0 for six-inch squid. Slide on a sleeve, a one-ounce egg sinker, and a squid. Check hook placement before crimping the sleeve to hold the squid in the proper location. This is followed by another sleeve, egg sinker, squid, etc. I space 14" between the first and second squid followed by 12" thereafter. There is no rule stating this is the proper distance. It just works for me. I know fishermen who use anywhere from six to 30" spacing. Finish the leader off with a double loop.

If you want the chain to skip and skim constantly on the surface, use corks or floats in place of egg sinkers. I have had success rigging this chain with floats in each of the squid except the last one, which has an egg sinker. When trolled, the first five squid are on the surface dancing with the last one working and diving beneath the surface in cleaner water.

Only your imagination limits you to the type of daisy chain pulled behind the boat. Just about any type of skirt can be rigged similar to the squid and achieve great results in the spread.

Pulled by themselves or in combination with rig baits, tuna clones and feathers are deadly.

TUNA CLONES AND FEATHERS

Although the name suggests their use for tuna, they can be deadly on just about any pelagic species and are responsible for many of my charters' fish thrown in the box over the years. The options here are many. These lures are available in an array of color schemes and finishes. Green/yellow, blue/white and black/purple are my favorites. Just about every manufacturer of offshore trolling lures has their own brand or twist to these lures. Heads may be made of chrome or diamond patterns to add flash. Two brands I routinely pull with success are Eye Catcher and Zuker. Both can be rigged and trolled as an artificial or used as a skirt over a ballyhoo. They also may be rigged as a daisy chain in the same manner as the cedar plug. These lures are on the small side, normally at six inches in length. Rig on 100-pound leader material with a 7/0 hook.

To explain all of the various artificial lures available to an angler would take up several volumes of books. Before going any further, it is important to understand that an angler must believe in his or her bait. I have no scientific formula nor can explain how or why believing in your bait makes a difference. However, it does! Once you find a bait that works for you, it is always going to work at one time or another. Maybe not every

Spoons can be just as productive offshore as they are when inshore and bay fishing.

time when offshore, but it becomes a standard by which you will measure all other bait performance. It will be in your starting point, depending on species that are being chased on any given day offshore. What works for another angler with great success may only provide mediocre results for you. Trial and error are the only ways for you to determine how to catch fish on what type of bait. Information contained in this book and knowledge you gather from fishermen or other fishing sources will be the starting point for acquiring the necessary skills to catch fish consistently. With that being said, trying to balance or fit everything into your boat may be difficult, but do not leave the dock without...

SPOONS

If I were only given one lure I could take offshore each day the spoon would be up for consideration. It is extremely versatile. This is proven time and time again by the many types of fish that try to consume it! Actually, I do not know any fish which, under the correct circumstances, are not fooled by this lure. Commonly used inshore for stripers, blues, and other species, its use offshore is overlooked by many bluewater fishermen. The lure is universal in that it may be trolled, cast, or even jigged. When captains and mates gather around the watering hole after long days offshore discussing what did or did not work, the spoon normally surfaces in the conversation. The decision on which type to purchase is not easy, with choices including Tony, Hopkins, Johnson, Clark, and others. I can share with you that, after years of trying all the previously mentioned pieces of metal, Drone spoons produce the most consistent results. This spoon in a size three and a half can handle speeds up to eight or nine knots and is deadly on bluefin, kings, wahoo and other tuna, depending on how it is rigged and the position it's trolled in the spread. White is the most consistent color producer, followed by silver. Red works well when trolled near the surface for kings. Remember, when picking out color choices keep in mind what was discussed under the color section. The color red is not going to be visible much below 10'.

There are days when tuna refuse to feed on the surface. This is when a Drone on a planer is your best friend. Used in conjunction with a planer, these spoons are ideal for targeting a depth where fish are being marked on the fish finder. If you have spent any amount of time offshore, you have heard this statement on the radio many times: "I'm marking fish down deep." A bell or light should be going off in your head, at this point. This is the indicator that tells you to go down and get them if fish are not feeding on the surface. The larger the planer size, the greater the depth obtained with a reasonable amount of line out. 50 class outfits can handle up to a number four planer, anything larger, and an 80 class outfit is necessary.

The other alternative is to run a planer off a dedicated line attached to a cleat or to the stern. For detailed use of planers application, they are covered under chapter 7. Large in-line sinkers are also able to be used in conjunction with spoons, but faster trolling speeds require heavier weight than in bay fishing. In-line sinkers weighting 28 ounces work well in most situations. However you get it down there, remember: always have a few of the incredible edible spoons to mix in your spread.

CHUGGERS

Moldcraft produces a line of lures which are called chuggers. Several other companies also manufacture this style of lure, with a head that has a flat or concave surface that causes splashing, diving, and movement to entice fish to strike. For our purposes we will throw all these lures into the category of chuggers. Available in a variety of sizes and styles, each has

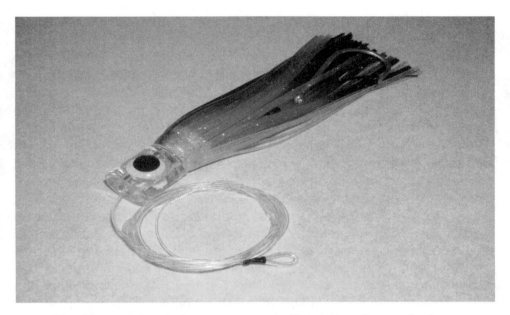

The flat heads of chuggers create fish-attracting splashes.

its own personality when trolled. As the clock of time turned into the 21st century these lures became popular and are used every day by offshore experts and weekend warriors. A mixture of these lures manufactured by Boone, Zuker, Moldcraft or C&H assures a variety in your spread. At one time or another I have found lures made by each of these companies productive. They catch fish rigged independently or when used in conjunction with rigged baits. If being rigged for white marlin, keep leader poundage to the light side, around 80- to 100- pounds. For tuna fishing and general trolling 130- to 150-pound leader is adequate. Large chuggers for blue marlin, should be rigged on 250-pound leader or higher. Use the appropriate size hook for the lure being rigged. Remember to keep the hook inside of the skirt and not protruding past the end.

RUBBER BALLYHOO

Natural or artificial ballyhoo? There was a time I would have scoffed at the notion that a rubber imitation ballyhoo would out-fish a natural rigged ballyhoo. That is, until I had the experience. On a day when there appeared to be absolutely nothing alive in the Atlantic Ocean, I rigged a couple Bullyhoo made by Calcutta baits and the yellowfin turned on! Before continuing the discussion of these baits, it is important to understand that I just introduced an unknown variable into the equation of catching fish—did the fish just decide to start biting, or was it changing over to a different bait that turned the bite on and was responsible for throwing five fish in the box? I've wrestled with this dilemma since beginning to fish offshore. I try not to dwell on this issue or allow it to consume all my waking moments. But, the important fact remains that a way was found to catch fish and the charter debarked with smiles on their faces. Regardless of the method or on what bait our charters catch fish, the end result and number one priority is to throw fish in the kill box. This is also the number one thought for most recreational anglers running offshore. As all anglers, knowing the answer as to what makes fish bite is a question certainly worth solving.

For the purpose of trying to understand the answer, let us divert from the use of Bullyhoo for a moment and look at inshore fishing, where bait is not always changed to entice fish to bite. Using flounder fishing as an example, the fish begin feeding because of a tide change. Anglers may sit for hours anchored or drifting without so much as a nibble, then the flounder turn on and feed for two hours. This type of fishing has no worries about changing the color or size of the bait, trolling lure distance from the transom, etc. The fish begin to bite when they are damn good and ready, normally during the last and beginning hour of a tide change. Does the

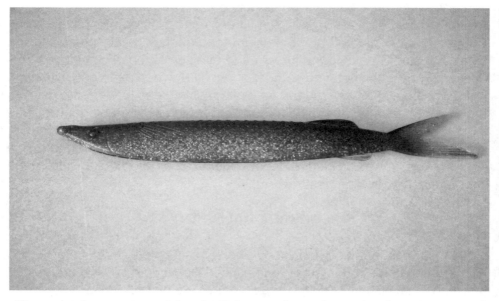

Many anglers carry rubber ballyhoo onboard as a backup to natural ballyhoo. Do not sell these short in their fish-catching ability.

same thing occur offshore? My conclusion is yes. Being at the right place at the right time is crucial to catching fish. Unfortunately, we do not have a tidal chart for offshore waters and are at the mercy of the currents. But, do we or do we not have some control over the bite? The bait offering, appearance and freshness certainly make a difference, however, the fish are not going to eat until they are ready. Can we entice a feeding period? Possibly for a fish or two, by changing the method or offering. Now, with that being said, I offer this rule: if what you are doing is not working, try something different! Since we are not certain what is occurring under the water's surface at any given time, trolling a variety of bait or colors may make a difference. I have starting lineups to begin trolling each day depending on species targeted (trolling patterns are covered under chapter 6). Your starting lineup is what normally produces the most fish. While it is always a good idea to begin with what has worked in the past, do not become trapped into not trying something different. No fish? Change the bait offering, patterns, color of skirts, etcetera. If lines do not come tight, begin to make changes. Dig out lures that have not seen the light of day for years, experiment with multiple skirts, leader weights and lengths. Change anything that possibly could make a difference. This includes trolling speed, and direction to current or seas. Finally, if nothing seems to work, return to your original fish-catching pattern.

Now, to get back to the topic of using Bullyhoo—the yellowfin were caught that day due to changing four lines over from natural rigged ballyhoo to imitation rubber Bullyhoo. The fish possibly would have taken naturals, but with lines coming tight, Bullyhoos were kept on them. There are several manufacturers of rubber ballyhoo. Carry a few packs for days when fishing is so phenomenal that you run out of naturals or, for those days they out-fish natural bait.

ILANDER

Ilander has designed several styles and types of fish-catching artificial lures. I have used several of the designs and find three extremely productive. No tackle chest is complete without a few of these proven fish catchers. First, a blue/white standard Ilander used as a skirt over a medium or large bally is right at the top of the list when it comes to a tuna bait. The combination is really too large for white marlin, but that does not stop them from attacking it. Blue marlin and dolphin also find the rig appetizing. On dark overcast days or early mornings when the sun is low in the sky, try using the black/purple color scheme. I have found this same lure in the crystal color deadly for tuna when feeding on squid. Next in line is the Jr. Ilander.

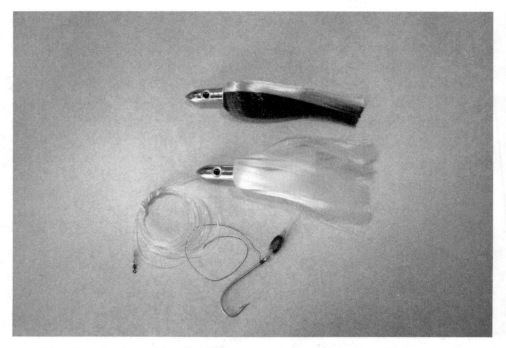

The llander in a blue/white or crystal color is deadly on tuna.

Use in combination with small or medium ballyhoo, in the same colors as its big brother. The lure produces well on flat lines, or any other position for that matter. Finally, the Sea Star model has produced tuna in the aforementioned colors and also blue/pink.

MANN G50+

If wahoo is on your wish list, this is a lure that should be considered for use in a mixed spread where you would like to increase the possibility of catching one. The lure cannot be trolled fast when trolling a dedicated wahoo spread. However, it can handle six or seven knots, which makes it ideal for mixing in a spread of natural baits. This deep-running lure is not cheap, but it does produce. Even with its large size, it comes rigged on a wire line to prevent those razor sharp teeth from cutting the lure off. It can reach depths of 50' when pulled with 200' of 50-pound test line out.

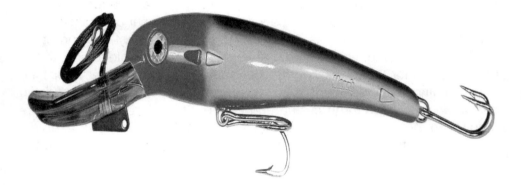

This is one lure Wahoo find difficult to pass up.

— CHAPTER FIVE —
NATURAL BAIT

Many times artificial lures are rigged in conjunction with natural bait to enhance performance. At other times, natural baits return better results rigged "naked," to appear in a natural swimming state. Either way, it is not advisable to count only on artificial lures or just rigged bait. Never cast off the dock lines without having an assortment of both on board. Which natural bait to use? The list is actually not that long, there are naturals that have been used for years and certainly will be used for years to come. The information provided is what works for me and should only be a starting point for this fascinating part of offshore fishing.

Rigging your own natural bait, compared to buying them pre-rigged, certainly gives a feeling of accomplishment when fish are caught on "your" bait. In addition, a lot of coin can be saved by rigging your own baits. If you want to use the freshest possible bait, learn to use a cast net and catch your own. Of course, with a limited amount of time available to fish, this is not an option for 95-percent of the fishermen who would rather be fishing then catching bait. This brings us to the second best option. Catch your own bait when time allows and pre-rig and freeze it for future use. If you take a day off of precious fishing time to catch bait, take the time to preserve it properly for future use. If done correctly, the bait can last throughout the fishing season.

FREEZING YOU OWN BAIT

Kosher salt, ice and a container are necessary when catching bait. Remember, fresh bait starts to deteriorate as soon as it comes out of the water. Mackerel, mullet, squid or bunker are all treated in the same respect. Use a cooler as a container, add one pound of kosher salt to each gallon of sea water, and mix in crushed/cubed ice to form a brine. You cannot use too much ice. The colder the brine, the better it preserves the bait. As bait is caught, handle it gently and place it in the salt brine. Once home, rig the baits and seal them in bags with a vacuum sealer. Place them in a deep freezer in a single layer. You want the bait to freeze as quickly as possible to preserve freshness.

The bait may be rigged after thawing. However, taking the time to rig baits when fresh and then freezing is the better way to go. No vacuum sealer available? Larger bait such as mullet or mackerel may be flash-frozen. Place the bait in a single layer in the freezer, on wax paper. Once frozen, remove and dip it in water. This forms a thin layer of ice over the bait. Place it back in the freezer for an hour and repeat the process. The bait can then be placed in zipper-lock bags and stored. The ice prevents air from reaching the baits and drying them out or causing freezer burn. The aforementioned procedure is best performed when your wife is not around the house!

PURCHASING FROZEN BAIT

The majority of fishermen buy frozen bait. With the exception of squid, the eyes are the first to indicate if the bait was taken care of when caught. If too much time was taken between catching and freezing the fish, the eyes become stained with blood around the sockets. The eyes should also be clear and not milky colored. Baitfish color fades once death occurs, but there should be no yellow coloring around the fins or belly area. This indicates a slow process of freezing or re-frozen bait. The packages should have no signs of frozen blood or excess fluid, which also indicates the bait was re-frozen. And by no means should the vacuum sealed package have any air!

Squid should be white in color and not pink, an indication of coming in contact with fresh water or growing old before freezing. Always thaw bait fish in saltwater, as freshwater softens the flesh. Actually, just being frozen softens the flesh of fish. After rigging frozen bait such as ballyhoo or mullet, they may be placed in a salt solution to toughen them back up. Magic Brine, Brine-n-Bait and other salt compounds which are mixed with water produce a solution to increase durability. Adding baking soda is said to preserve the color. I have tried this and personally could not tell any difference, but I include it since many anglers swear that it makes a difference. You may want to give it a try. Kosher salt works about as well as any commercial brine I have tried. Rig baits and place in a mixture of one half pound salt to one gallon of seawater. Mix in ice to form the brine.

Mackerel and mullet have softer flesh then ballyhoo and receive the greatest benefit from this process. I do not place ballyhoo that are in good condition in a brine solution. Ballyhoo, depending on speed being trolled, can last an hour or more before having the bottom cavity blow out. Once rigged, if ballyhoo are not in prime condition they may be put in a brine solution or toughened up by directly covering with kosher salt for an hour. However, do not allow them to dry out and become stiff, which may present a spinning problem when trolled.

baits are rigged they need to be stored for use. I have never had the fortunate pleasure of a refrigerated bait box onboard any of my boats nor charter boats I have worked. This meant a small cooler was dedicated as a bait box. A tight fitting lid in the 28-quart size provides all the room necessary. Two blocks of ice fit neatly in the bottom. Over the ice place a piece of cardboard or aluminum foil to prevent the bait from coming in contact with fresh water from the ice. If salting of the bait is necessary, it can be accomplished right in the bait box.

A description of each bait and rigging technique follows. Keep in mind, every captain or mate has their own little twist to rigging each type of bait. I have included the tricks that have worked for me over the years.

SEA WITCHES

Before examining the different types of natural baits to rig naked, more often then not, natural baits are skirted. This prolongs the life of the bait along with adding color. The C&H Sea Witch is without a doubt the

A bait box containing an ample supply of pinless ballyhoo for the day ahead.

most popular skirt used to add color to rigged bait. It comes in different weights and is sized correctly for medium to large ballyhoo. They also work as skirts for other rigged naturals for adding color. If used on small naturals, the skirt may be trimmed so the bait does not become lost. Blue/white is a favorite color for general use. Red/white serves well for billfish as does pink and multicolored. Dolphin seem to be partial to the yellow/chartreuse. Actually, I do not believe any of their color choices can serve you wrong. Similar skirts are available from several different companies. All seem to work well. Skirts such as the Eyecatcher brand create a lot of flash. Eyecatchers also flare open when coming out of the water which adds fish appeal. It is the added color to the rigged bait, however, which I believe makes fish attack on certain days.

Stick to the dark colors on cloudy or overcast days or when the sun is low on the horizon. Switch over to brighter skirts as the sun intensifies. One exception: fishing for wahoo, where the color of black/purple works during all periods of the day. The majority of the naturals trolled in my spread are skirted unless strictly bill fishing, in which case most naturals are left naked.

BALLYHOO

Responsible for catching every species that swims in the ocean, they are the number one bait to troll. Ballyhoo are the mainstay of offshore natural bait. Versatility in rigging allows the bait to perform in different manners, from skipping on to diving under the surface. Regardless of how the bait is rigged, it needs to be pre-prepped.

The following methods of rigging ballyhoo work, period. With that said, my recommendations are not the only way to rig the baits. Walk along the charter dock any evening and you will observe four people rigging ballyhoo four different ways. Everyone has their own special twist. This does not mean it is the only correct or right way to rig the bait. However, every person who rigs ballyhoo has the same objective: to make the bait swim and appear natural in the water. Keep in mind when reading the different methods of rigging that one fact remains constant, the ballyhoo must be "pulled" from the front or bill area of the fish. If the hook is tight against the skin of the stomach, the ballyhoo is going to spin. A ballyhoo being pulled with tension against the hook in the body cavity is the number one reason for spinning, and a spinning bait does not catch fish!

A prime example of this dilemma is when marlin fishing and using ballyhoo as pitch-baits. The bait must swim properly as soon as it hits the water, and only proper rigging allows the bait to perform. Your rigging method becomes very serious after your first pitch-bait spins and a marlin swims away! Number one rule, learn to keep the hook loose in the body cavity and spinning becomes almost non-existent. Second, a bait made stiff by salting may also spin upon hitting the water. Never salt a pitch-bait. The ballyhoo must be thawed before rigging. The first step is to remove the eyes; they may be left in if being skirted. But the eyes fill with water and balloon out if being trolled naked, preventing the ballyhoo from swimming correctly. By removing the eyes, rigging also becomes easier. An added benefit of removing eyes is that the bait smokes when trolled. This is caused by air bubbles formed from the empty eye cavities. The shaft of an old aluminum arrow works well for removing eyes.

Next, the waste from the intestines and stomach must be removed. This step is skipped by some anglers and they still have a ballyhoo that swims naturally when rigged. However, by removing the innards, there is less adjusting necessary. Lay the ballyhoo on a flat surface. Place your

An arrow shaft works well for removing ballyhoo eyes.

thumb behind the head on the body cavity/stomach area and push towards the tail while using slight pressure. The innards and waste comes out the anus. Do not apply a lot of pressure, you do not want to remove the scales which make the bait flash. It may take two or three passes to remove everything.

Next step is to make the back flexible. The back bone is not broken but the scales which support the spine of the fish are "popped." Use the thumb and forefinger to pinch along the spine from the head towards the tail. You must be careful not to apply too much pressure which can cause the skin of the ballyhoo to tear. After a little practice you will learn to pop the spine. This step is the difference between having a ballyhoo appear to "swim" or just be pulled through the water.

Once the back is popped the ballyhoo can be bent and made flexible. Once again, be careful not to tear the skin on the bait when bending. Bend slowly to prevent this from occurring.

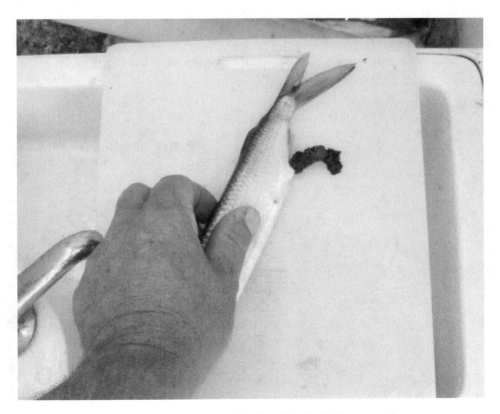

Removing the waste helps the ballyhoo swim.

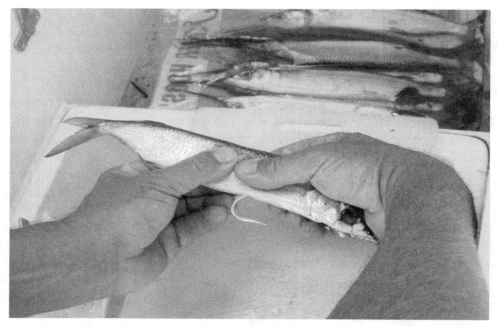

The spine can be "popped" before or after rigging.

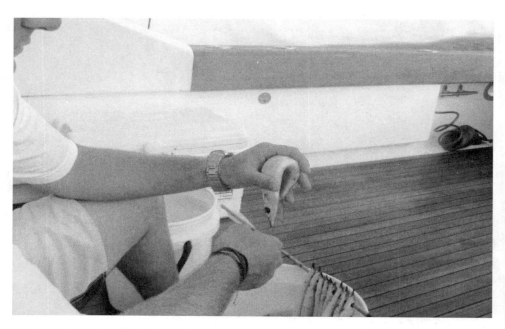

Bending the ballyhoo keeps a natural appearance when rigged.

PINLESS BALLYHOO RIG

The pinless rig allows a ballyhoo to be trolled naked, skirted or used in conjunction with lures. Medium and large ballyhoo appear to be actually swimming when rigged properly. Small size ballyhoo do not obtain the action of the larger bait, but do not discount them. Certain days marlin and tuna prefer a small bait over a large. The pinless rig may not provide the durability of a pinned rig (discussed next) when attacked by billfish, nonetheless, they are easy to rig and may be used in most situations. Wind-on or a standard leader is your choice as discussed in chapter 3. Mustad hook #3407 work well in the 6/0 size for small ballyhoo, 7/0 for medium and depending on the size of large ballyhoo, an 8/0 or 9/0 serves the purpose.

The hook and a ¼ to ½-ounce egg sinker get crimped to the end of 100-pound monofilament leader, or your poundage of choice. A piece of rigging wire, either stainless or copper, is wrapped around the shank of the hook and brought up through the hook's eye. I prefer copper over stainless wire since the brightness of stainless wire stands out after rigging. Copper rigging wire is sold in pre-cut lengths of nine and 13" lengths. Do not waste your time with the nine inch. 13" works in most situations. But the best

The pinless rig is ideal for use on naked or skirted ballyhoo.

option is to buy a 200' roll of Malin rigging wire. This assures you always have a piece long enough to finish the job. Nothing is more annoying then to need two more inches of rigging wire to finish up. The egg sinker can be eliminated if the bait is to be skipped on the surface or when trolled slow, as in three or four knots.

Lay the ballyhoo on its side and decide where the hook must protrude through the stomach cavity so the egg sinker fits under the gill plate. Then run the hook in under a gill plate and work it to the location where it is to exit the body cavity.

Try to keep the hook as low in the body as possible to assist the bait in swimming correctly. If the hook is inserted high near the backbone, the high position and the hook's weight can cause a problem in the natural swimming ability of the bait.

It is extremely important that the hook not pull against the body of the bait where it exits or it will not swim correctly. A small slit can be inserted where the hook exits in the body cavity if desired. Once the hook is inserted, set the sinker up in the gills.

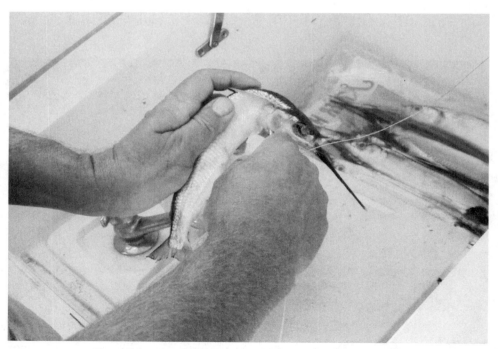

Bending the ballyhoo helps to insert a hook.

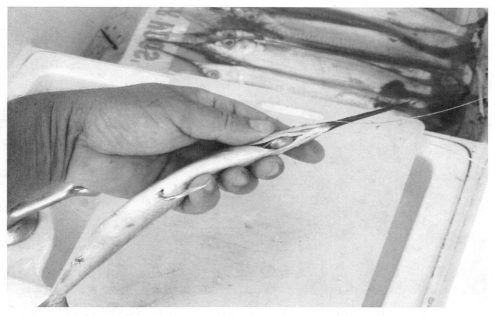

The weight must be centered in the gill plates for the ballyhoo to swim naturally.

Go through the eye sockets with the rigging wire and pull the hook snug. Make two wraps under the head and back through the eye sockets to hold the gills shut. One wrap in front of the sinker, one behind. Once again, pull the wire to snug up the hook after making the wraps.

Push the rigging wire from the bottom of the fish up through the bill, coming out at the base of the mouth on top the head. The top mouth of a ballyhoo has a hinged section close to the head which allows the wire to penetrate with ease. Only practice teaches this location and simplifies securing a ballyhoo onto the hook with just a rigging wire. Wrap the rigging wire two times around the bill. Go through the eye socket and back across the top of the head. If done correctly, the top of the ballyhoo should look like an X to hold the mouth shut and secure the bait to the hook.

Finish by wrapping 1/3 of the way down the bill, then back up. Break off the excess bill so it does not interfere with the lure or skirt. If the ballyhoo is to be trolled naked, do not break the bill off, but wrap the rigging wire to the end of the bill with the line under the bill. This allows the bait to swim naturally by being pulled from the front of the bill. A rigged ballyhoo ready to be skirted and catch fish should appear something like in the photo.

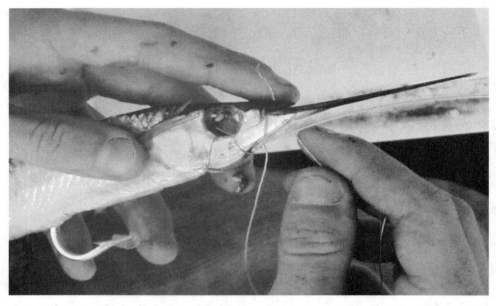

Learning to rig ballyhoo with just a rigging wire makes for the most natural presentation.

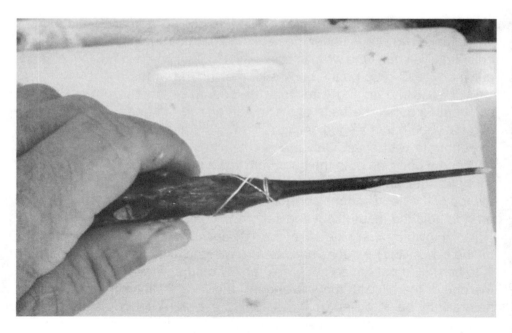

The top of a properly rigged ballyhoo should appear to be an X.

A properly pinless rigged ballyhoo.

PIN BALLYHOO RIG

Many anglers learning to rig ballyhoo for offshore fishing find inserting a rigging wire through the head of a ballyhoo somewhat difficult. Once mastered, it is my recommendation for rigging. However, to speed up the process, anglers may want to construct their ballyhoo rig by utilizing a pin. This pin system can be used with a rigging wire or a nose spring to hold the ballyhoo to the rig, instead of a rigging wire. The pin is made from a piece of number 12 or 15 wire bent at a 90-degree angle and crimped along with the hook to the leader. If an egg sinker is desired, slide it on before crimping the wire. Be sure the wire pin is aligned with the hook. This assures the ballyhoo is pulled straight through the water.

If the pin rig is to be used for a naked presentation, secure the ballyhoo to the rig with rigging wire, which is less visible then the nose spring. The pin rig may also be used with a rubber band to hold the ballyhoo to the rig. I know several anglers who use this method. I do not care for the rubber band system, but you may want to give it a try. Rigging with a nose spring is a piece of cake, just twist the wire onto the protruding pin coming out of the head until the bally-hoo snugs tight. This rig is ideal for use with a skirt since the nose spring is concealed and flares out skirts. The spring also makes for fast re-rigging. However there is a drawback; it does not hold the gill plates closed, which can cause problems in swimming ability when not skirted.

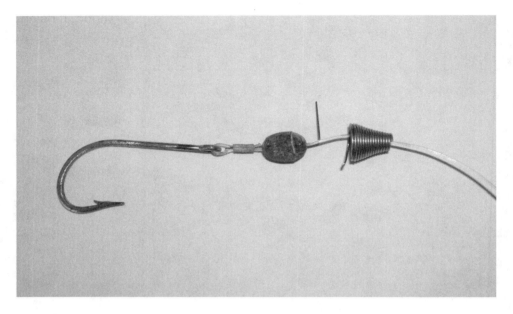

The pin wire runs through the egg sinker and is crimped along with the hook. Be sure to allow a little room for the sinker to move. This allows for slight error when rigging or setting the hook in the bally-hoo and allows the sinker to be adjusted accordingly.

A ballyhoo rigged with a nose spring.

The pin rig may be used with wire in place of a nose spring. If using wire, wrap in the same fashion as with a pinless rig. The only exception is the wire is not pushed through the head and out the top of the mouth, since the pin already goes through here. I prefer using wire over a nose spring since the wire locks the egg sinker in the gills.

The pin rig, using rigging wire.

SPLIT BILL RIG

The split bill rig allows the ballyhoo to swim under the surface and provides the most lifelike action. A downfall is that every piece of floating grass you troll by catches on the bill. Rigging ballyhoo in this fashion requires constant attention to the bait. And, the split bill does not allow for trolling fast. However, for trolling up to six knots it is a winner for taking fish.

To rig one, utilize the aforementioned method for the pinless rig. Prep the ballyhoo as previously mentioned, but add this additional step. Hold the bill of the ballyhoo between the thumb and forefinger. Twirl the bill back and forth between your fingers, and the bill will split in half in the middle, lengthwise. The bill may also be cut with a knife or even your thumb nail is capable of splitting the bill.

Measure and place the hook in the body cavity and secure the hook with the standard rigging practice previously explained. After rigging the hook in the body cavity, place the leader between the separated bill sections, tight against the rigging wraps. Continue wrapping past the leader to

With a little practice the bill can be separated by twirling between the fingers.

the end of the bill. When trolled, the bill on the ballyhoo acts like the lip on a diving plug and constantly digs. This method of rigging provides a lot of action to the bait. This bait attracts even the most skittish of fish into striking.

Split bill ballyhoo are very popular for sailfish. Normally when rigging for sails and many times for white marlin, ballyhoo are rigged using a short shank hook such as a Mustad 9174. Rig in the same method as a longer shank hook. Insert the hook under a gill plate and thread into the body cavity. Make sure the hook is dead center when it comes out of the body. You will find the short shank hook is easier to work into the body compared to longer shank hooks. It is important in all ballyhoo rigging that the hook remains stable. Remember, if the hook pulls against the body cavity, the bait does not swim correctly. If using short shank hooks, finish off exactly as stated for a split bill using a longer shank.

You will develop a preference for a short on longer shank hook for rigging ballyhoo. Both work in all ballyhoo rigging situations. A short shank hook allows the bait to swim better, but I feel longer shank hooks have just a slight advantage when it comes to hook-up percentage, especially when billfishing.

This is the ballyhoo rig most likely to attract skittish fish.

The amount of weight necessary is consistent with your trolling speed. When trolling around four knots for sails or even white marlin, ballyhoo swim without any weight if rigged properly. As speed increases ¼- or ½-ounce egg sinkers keeps the bait running true and straight. Large ballyhoo may require up to one ounce to prevent the bait from turning on its side when trolled upwards of six knots. If the bait is swimming on its side, the problem may also be that the hook is misaligned and not in the middle of the body, or the weight is off-center under the gills. Anytime a ballyhoo does not appear natural, wind it in and adjust it so it swims correctly. Many times it is faster to rig a new bait then try to straighten out one that has been rigged incorrectly.

CIRCLE HOOK BALLYHOO RIGS

If you are targeting billfish on your offshore pursuits, consider rigging with circle hooks, from a conservation standpoint. If you intend to fish marlin tournaments it appears circle hooks will be mandatory in some cases. This book is going to the publisher before the Highly Migratory Species Division of the National Marine Fisheries Service (NMFS) decides whether or not to place a five year moratorium on the catching of White Marlin beginning in 2007. The moratorium does allow for catch and release. Assuming this moratorium passes, rigging with circle hooks is the way of the future for billfishing in tournament situations.

Mexico and the Caribbean receive a lot of criticism concerning the harvesting of billfish by recreational fishermen chartering in these areas. While many of the captains and mates sell billfish, mainly blue marlin, to supplement their incomes, I would be remiss if I did not give credit to those fishermen from these areas who insist upon catch and release. Many began using circle hooks for billfish long before it became popular here in on the east coast.

As in all rigging situations, there are several ways to rig a circle hook with a ballyhoo. I have included two proven methods. First, do not use or make a circle hook offset, it only makes the ballyhoo harder to track. The first method is the easiest. It does not allow for fast trolling since no weight is utilized. Use a circle hook appropriate for the size ballyhoo. Attach the hook to a leader with a crimp or if using light leader, it may be tied using your favorite knot. I use an Improved Clinch knot for this application since I prefer the hook to be stationary to the leader.

Prep the ballyhoo in the normal fashion. Use a rigging wire and wrap around the shank of the hook, bringing the wire out through the eye of the hook. Push the rigging wire up through the lower jaw and come out the hinge on the top of the mouth.

Pull the hook snug under the ballyhoo. Wire the gills closed while at the same time securing the hook. You do not want the hook to move. Finish by wrapping the wire around the bill in the normal rigging fashion. Rigged properly, the ballyhoo trolls naturally.

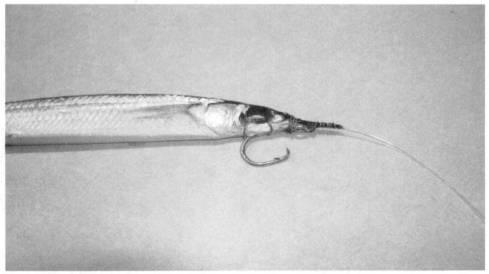

A properly rigged, weightless circle hook ballyhoo is an ideal sail-fish bait.

There are situations where anglers want to increase trolling speed. This requires rigging utilizing an egg sinker. Using a piece of rigging wire, form a haywire twist loosely around the hook. You want the hook to be free to swivel. Begin at the base of the top of the mouth and run the wire down through the hinge in the jaw, and out the bottom of the head. Then, slide an egg sinker on the rigging wire.

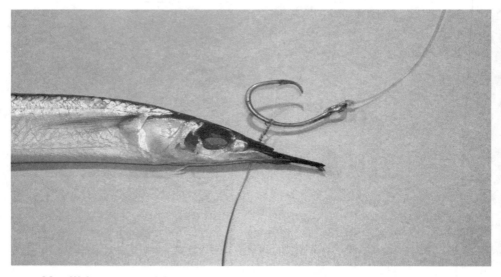

You'll have to add an egg sinker to increase trolling speeds.

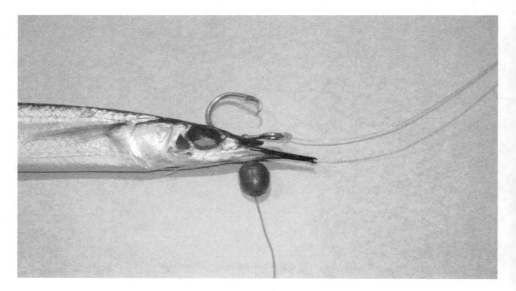

Slide the egg sinker onto the wire.

Pull the rigging wire until the haywire twist snugs to the top of the head. The haywire twist needs to be exposed to allow the hook to move. Locate the egg sinker up in the gills and using the rigging wire, secure the gills closed by going through the eyes in front and back of the sinker. Finish by wrapping the leader to the bill and snap off the excess bill.

Remember—when using circle hook rigs never set the hook, just wind the line tight.

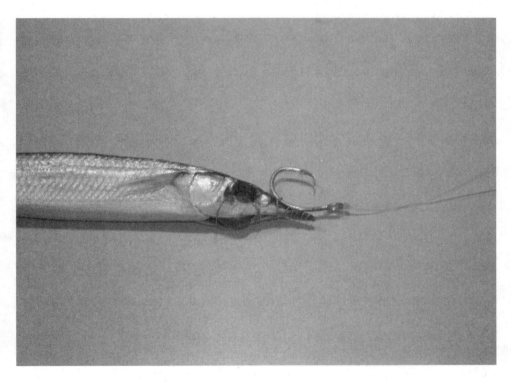

The finished product.

MULLET

Anglers that use mullet on a regular basis find it hard to run offshore without having them onboard. Like the ballyhoo, everything in the ocean eats mullet. But, with that being said, probably less than 10 percent of the boats pull a mullet in the spread. I suspect this is due to the time required to rig mullet. Unlike rigging ballyhoo after catching a fish or when needing to be replaced, the same rig is not used. Mullet are rigged individually. After a bite or when a replacement is needed, a new pre-rigged mullet with leader is attached to the line. There really is no shortcut when it comes to rigging. I know anglers who rig mullet in the fashion of ballyhoo, and I've tried this but did not find satisfactory results. If you're going to fish with mullet, re-solve yourself to the fact that it is going to be more time consuming than ballyhoo. But, the extra time is more than worthwhile. Of course mullet can be purchased pre-rigged. But even with these, most of the time tweaking is necessary.

The size offering of mullet seems to be the main factor that indicates whether or not it is devoured by pelagics. I've touched on the feeding style of many species in chapter 10, Targeted Species. Feeding style may be a factor why the size of mullet, ballyhoo or any natural bait for that matter, makes a difference in the amount of bites received. Yellowfin and bluefin tuna, for example, inhale prey when feeding. Even though their mouth is certainly large enough to inhale just about any size bait trolled, when feeding on smaller baitfish, they may shy away from larger baits that are difficult to swallow. Whereas wahoo have no problem attacking large bait since their method of feeding is grabbing and biting the prey, often cutting it in half before finishing off the meal. It is always a good idea to carry an assortment of bait sizes when running offshore. You may not always be able to match what is being fed upon, but if eight-inch tinker mackerel are showing up in stomachs, the same size mullet or artificial lures normally suffices.

There are two ways to rig mullet, whole or split tail. Personally I prefer the split tail mullet which gets better action and can be rigged with double hooks, increasing chances of hook-ups. But, both make an excellent trolled bait that offshore predators find hard to pass up.

SPLIT TAIL MULLET

In chapter 3 I discussed single-strand wire leader and mentioned it still has application even with the arrival of fluorocarbon leaders on the fishing scene. Mullet can be rigged on fluorocarbon or monofilament. However, single strand wire leader is ideal for the job. Most anglers use Mustad 3407 hooks in a size to match the mullet, which mostly ranges from 7/0 to 9/0. A split tail rig needs decent size hooks. Smaller hooks tend to become lost in the body and may become fouled. If the hooks you decide to use when rigging mullet appear on the small side, they probably are—move up one size. Before explaining the rigging process, it is probably beneficial to see exactly what a split tail rig looks like without the mullet. Keep in mind, this rig is constructed after the hooks are placed inside the mullet. The only pre-rigging that may be done beforehand is putting the two hooks together in tandem.

The first step is to prepare the mullet for rigging. Since this is more time-consuming than prepping ballyhoo, anglers may want to do this the night before fishing unless fishing the northeast, where there is probably ample time running to fishing grounds. Although, since a sharp knife will be in hand and precise cuts are necessary, unless you're fortunate enough to be fishing off a battlewagon or have flat seas, prepping probably should be

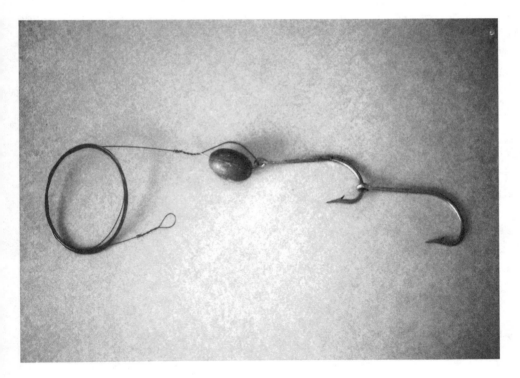

Notice the haywire twist for connecting to a swivel. A 100-pound Spro barrel swivel may be used if a wind-on leader is desired.

done on shore.

A sharp, thin-blade knife is necessary to split the tail. Cut along the backbone towards the tail. Now this is where it gets a little tricky. Holding the knife at a slight downward angle, cut through the middle of the tail. If done properly, the mullet's tail splits evenly in half. To perform splitting the tail, the mullet must be on a smooth surface.

Once this cut is mastered, rigging split tail mullet becomes a piece of cake. Use the knife and remove the majority of the meat and all the bones off both skins. The rest of the backbone needs to be removed. This may be done with a commercial de-boner or the shaft of an aluminum arrow. Insert your de-boner tool under one of the gills and into the backbone. Push to remove the bone. The next step is not completed by everyone rigging mullet, but I find that it helps the swimming ability. Make a ½" incision down through the top of the head beginning behind the eyes. Once this incision is made, lay the mullet on a flat surface. Take the palm of your hand and press down on the side of the head making it flat. The mullet is now prepped and ready to be rigged. If the mullet was not fresh, but thawed for rigging, it may be prudent to salt the mullet down to toughen it up. Thawed

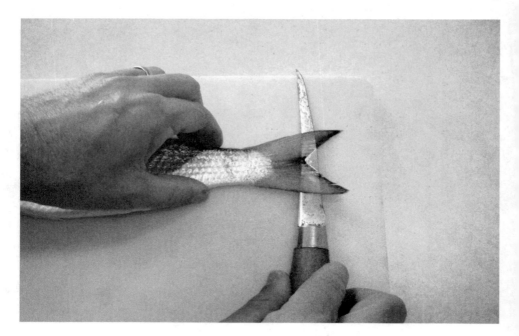

Splitting the tail on a mullet is not as difficult as it looks.

mullet tend to be mushy.

Anywhere from a one- to two-ounce egg sinker is necessary for rigging, depending on the bait size. Begin by measuring where the first hook will protrude through the stomach. When taking this measurement, imagine the eye of the hook just inside the mouth of the mullet. Make the incision in the stomach for the hook. Now, place the hooks into the body cavity and work the eye of the first hook up into the mouth of the fish. The first hook should protrude through the incision you made in the bottom of the stomach. The second hook should come to where the tail is split. It may be necessary to split the tail farther so the second hook rides properly. Slide the egg sinker onto the wire leader. Insert wire through the bottom of the mouth, the eye of the hook, and come out the top of the head. Snug the egg sinker under the jaw, while taking the tag end of the wire leader and finish off with a haywire twist in front of the egg sinker. The egg sinker should sit under the mullet's chin.

The final step is tying a piece of Dacron or waxed line around the head to keep the gills shut. A properly rigged split tail mullet should appear as follows.

A properly rigged spilt tail.

WHOLE RIGGED MULLET

Rigging a whole mullet is not quite as complicated as a split tail. Prepping the bait consist of removing the back bone. Work your de-boning tool under the gill, down through the fish getting as close as possible to the end of the tail. If the whole backbone is not removed the bait does not swim properly. Many anglers cut a hole in the top of the head in order to insert the de-boner into the fish and remove the backbone. I frown upon this as it allows water to enter the bait when trolled, which at times causes problems with presentation. Stick with de-boning from under the gill. Once the backbone is removed, make a small incision in the top of the head and flatten it for better swimming ability. The bait is now ready to be rigged.

Whole mullet are rigged with one hook. It is advisable to use a hook slightly larger than what appears necessary. Take a measurement with the hook against the side of the mullet to locate where to make a stomach incision. Insert the hook in the body cavity through the incision and work the eye of the hook up into the mouth area. From this point on, rig identical as with a split tail mullet, making certain that the gills are tied shut tightly. Otherwise, water entering into the gills causes a problem while trolling.

SQUID

Is there a better bait then squid? I do not believe so. I previously wrote everything in the ocean eats ballyhoo and mullet. Which is true. But given a choice, I truly believe most pelagic are going to eat squid. All an angler has to do is check stomach contents. If squid are available, they are in the stomachs of every fish brought aboard. Then why do we not see more squid in trolling spreads? The answer is easy—they are a pain in the #$% to rig. I despised sitting in the pit for an hour each evening just to rig squid for the next day. I am not saying there is anything wrong with the time-proven rigging technique using a float, crimp, wax thread and sewing needle. However, the rigging method I am about to show is quick and produces the same results... fish! Also, I find that by using a sinker in place of the float, the squid runs underwater, producing better results. Someone always tries to come up with a better mouse trap. This is exactly what I did for rigging squid.

I like to use a short shank hook appropriate for the squid's size. Typically a 7/0 to 9/0 fits the bill. Begin constructing the rig by sliding a 3/4- to one-ounce egg sinker onto the leader and crimp on the hook. Crimp a wind-on swivel to the other end of the leader. The rig is complete! That's all there is to it with the exception of a piece of rubber band. Before rigging the

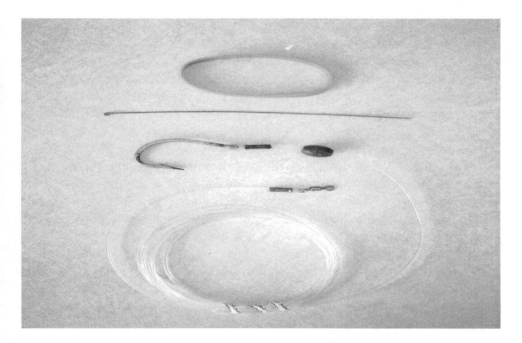

This is all that's necessary to rig squid quickly and easily.

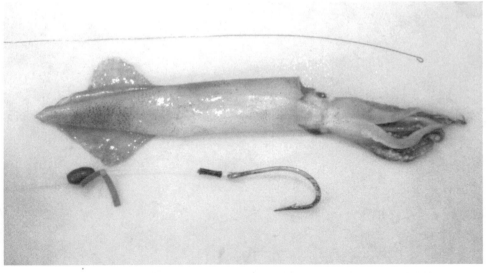

Take a measurement and tie a piece of rubber band to hold the egg sinker in the proper location.

squid, take a measurement so the egg sinker will be located just inside the squid and the hook will be in the head.

Use a piece of the rubber band and tie around the leader tightly to prevent the egg sinker from sliding down the leader. Take a piece of number 12 or 15 hard wire and using pliers, bend a very small hook into the end just large enough to hook the swivel.

Slide the wire up through the body of the squid and come out the top. Attach the swivel to the wire and slowly pull the swivel and leader through the body. The small swivel will pull right through the top of squid. Pull through remaining line until the egg sinker rests in the top of the squid. Insert the hook into the squid and the rig is ready to be fished. A half-dozen can be made up in little time. Changing bait only requires tying on a new rig to the leader for wind-on applications. Or, the swivel can be attached to a snap swivel if a standard double-line trolling setup is being used. If trolling in excess of six knots you may want to tie a piece of wax line or Dacron around the top of the squid to prevent it from sliding down over the egg sinker. However, this seldom is necessary.

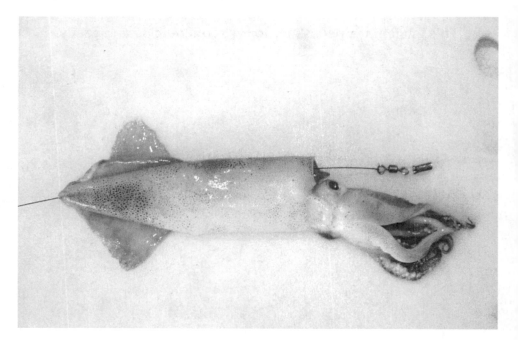

The line and swivel will slide easily through the squid.

The finished squid should appear like this.

RIGGING LIVE BAIT

Live bait fished for large pelagics can be the ticket for hook-ups. I use this rig when fishing bluefish off of a kite for mako. It also works well for rigging skipjack tuna for blue marlin. Remember when using a large bait to give time for the bait to be swallowed before setting the hook. The trick to rigging a live fish is to have everything ready before the bait is caught. It does not take very long to sap the friskiness out of a fish when it's out of the water and being rigged. The process can be accomplished well under a minute.

The rig consists of a leader with a hook crimped to the end. Allow room when crimping for the hook to swing freely. Do not crimp the line tight around the eye of the hook. Take a piece of heavy Dacron line, about 30" in length, and tie the ends together. Secure the Dacron to the hook. Also take a six-inch piece of number 15 wire and bend a small hook into one end. You are now ready to rig the baitfish when it comes onboard. First step in handling the baitfish is to place a wet towel around the fish and place the fish between the knees. Quickly push the wire through the top of an eye socket and out the top of the other eye socket. Make sure not to puncture the eyes. There is a hollow area over top and slightly forward of the eyes. It does not damage the fish inserting the wire. Hook the Dacron with the wire and pull the double line through the fish. Tie the Dacron to the hook. Make the hook snug, but not tight against the fish. The hook should be free to move. Place the fish into the water and attach the fishing line to a kite, or the fish can be allowed to swim around freely. The fish may also be SLOW trolled. Actually it is not trolling as much as keeping the boat straight while the fish swims behind. If you pull the fish, life expectancy is not good. Allow the fish to swim, and a properly rigged live bait can last for hours.

— CHAPTER SIX —
TROLLING

My theory has always been, "the more the better." I like my spread to present a variety of offerings in hopes of quickly finding the preferred bait of the day. Of course, the more lines you pull, the greater the chance for tangles when turning or once a fish is hooked up. It's a trade-off. Only with experimentation will you decide how many lines you feel comfortable trolling. If just beginning to dabble in offshore fishing, simplicity is a good starting point. Start with a basic five-line spread. This is the foundation upon which the building blocks of trolling may be added.

Professional captains such as Josh Rusky normally pull seven lines, which to me seems like a waste with a 13' cockpit width. However, with his success ratio, his technique has proven itself time and time again. I like a nine line spread. On slow days when the wind and water conditions allow, I up it to eleven. More lines in the water normally equal more headaches, but I find the benefits more often then not outweigh the trouble. Regardless of how many lines are placed in the water, proper spacing of the baits helps prevent lines from coming in contact with one another.

SPREADS

A five line spread consist of two flat lines, two rigger lines and a fifth line which may be alternated from the sweet spot, which is the location between the flat and rigger lines, and pulled in the way back position, trailing the rigger lines. The set up really depends on the type of fish being targeted. Chapter 10 discusses tips on line placement for each species when applicable.

A question most anglers have when setting lines is, "how far back?" Often you hear the distance referred to as waves. Such as, "place the bait between the forth and fifth wave." Depending on the size boat and speed, the distance changes and this may not be the best indicator for setting lines. At other times it's necessary to use waves for placement (I used the reference in this book earlier) because you want the bait or lure to ride in a specific position in relation to the wave sets.

Flat lines are normally set close to the boat. The average distances when setting these two lines are one at 25' and the other 35'. If a third flat line is run, I place it behind these, about 50' off the transom. This forms a pyramid or triangle of bait close to the boat.

Set the rigger lines in a five-rod setup at 100' and 150' respectfully.

This is a starting position set-up. If results are not favorable, meaning no bites, then the spread may be tightened up or stretched out. If running three flat lines, the first change to consider on a slow day is to relocate the center flat line and place it in the way back position. Way back means "way back." The bait is out of sight. Half a spool of line is dumped. Or if you prefer a yardage, place the bait 200-yards behind the boat. When you hear radio chatter refer to way, way back, you can figure the bait is 300-plus-yards behind the boat. However, this is not always practical. The amount of boats trolling a particular area dictates how far back the lines may be trolled.

Increasing the number of lines to seven is accomplished by adding two more outrigger lines. These are referred to as short riggers, and the other two rigger lines then are referred to as long riggers. A seven line spread is probably the most widely used spread and is often used with teasers, which are covered in the next section. Smaller boats may also be able to increase their number of lines by using clamp-on rod holders.

Regardless of how many lines are trolled it is imperative to space the lines in a manner that prevents entanglement on turns. This means if running very long lines, they need to swing in unison. This is accomplished by placing them the same distance from the boat. Another option is to place the longer line so it is able to swing overtop the shorter line when making turns. Use this rule of thumb when setting lines to help prevent tangles, "the longer the line...the higher the line."

TEASERS

Teasers are just what the name applies. They tease fish into coming behind the boat to examine activity. Most often used for billfish, who seem to have a curious manner, do not discount their use for raising other types of fish offshore. I normally use teasers and/or dredges (discussed next) whenever trolling, unless limited by the number of lines that can be placed in the water due to the boat's setup. Teasers normally are large in size or at least designed to make a large surface disturbance. They may be individual lures or daisy chain type lures but without hooks. Pulled off the outrigger, they normally have dedicated reels located where it is easy to control the teaser's action. This is especially important when billfishing and using the bait and switch tactic. No riggers? Teasers may be pulled off cleats or other positions on the boat as well. It is important to position bait around the teasers. Fish raised to teasers often switch over and attack bait more to their liking.

Years ago when it was necessary for me to count pennies in order to fish, our fishing budget did not allow for teasers (mine did, it was my wife's that didn't!) A simple teaser chain was made before venturing out each day. Five beer cans were placed on a length of 3/16" rope. It was amazing how many bluefin tuna this configuration raised. If you want to make a poor man's teaser, pick up five fender washers at the local hardware store. They are washers with small diameter center holes. The washer is necessary to prevent the cans from tearing through the knots that are to be tied. Tie a knot in the end of the teaser line and slide on a washer followed by a beer (soda?) can. Tie another knot a foot above the first and so forth until all five cans are on the line. The teaser can be pulled off of a cleat and churns up a remark-able amount of water. Place a cedar plug five feet behind the teaser and watch the action! The cans do not last for many trips offshore. However, with no cost factor they are a good substitute for costly store-bought teasers.

Often I use spreader bars without hooks as teasers when tuna fish-ing. By placing a lure or rigged natural bait a few feet behind the bar, a 30 or 50 class outfit can be used instead of an 80 class outfit, which is normally necessary to pull a spreader bar.

Try a "real" bowling pin teaser. At over three pounds, this teaser causes commotion that fish find difficult to pass up. Not available in stores, this is a self made teaser. I pulled the teaser religiously during the grand daddy of marlin tournaments, the 2006 White Marlin Open, held out of

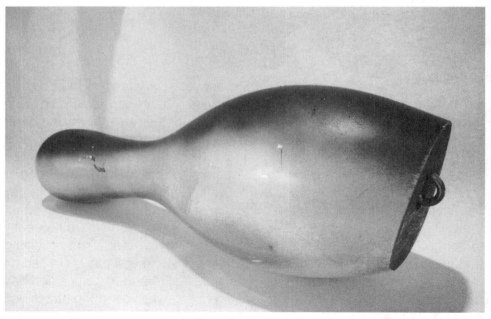

Teasers create a disturbance and draw the fish in.

Ocean City, Maryland. It raised two blue marlin during three days of fishing, and both fell to the bait and switch method using large ballyhoo. One blue, estimated at 350-pounds, could not resist the painted tuna configuration. However, Marlin are not the only species that find the teaser interesting. Yellowfin tuna are often observed swimming under the teaser before attacking ballyhoo on the short rigger and flat lines. On occasion, I place the teaser behind a dredge, imitating a tuna chasing bait fish. This trick works great for raising all types of fish.

In order to construct your own bowling pin teaser the first step is to locate a bowling pin. An inquiry at your local bowling alley may provide a pin. My local alley was more then glad to provide a few old ones free of charge. Another option is to conduct a search on Ebay. Used pins normally go for a buck or two. Once obtained, start by cutting a 30-degree angle across the bottom of the pin. A sharp blade is necessary since the pins are made of hard maple wood. Drill a pilot hole in the center, insert an eye hook screw, and spray paint the pin to your favorite color scheme.

DREDGES

If you plan on billfishing, then plan on buying or making a dredge. Like the teaser, it raises more then just billfish and can be used anytime when trolling offshore. A school of baitfish swimming behind the boat is an appetizing meal for any pelagic and this is just what the dredge imitates. When purchasing one, your wallet dictates how big a dredge is behind your boat. Pre-made dredges range from $75 up to several hundred dollars, depending on the amount and type of bait on the dredge.

Making your own dredge is not that difficult. There are three choices when it comes to dredges. A natural dredge, which is made from fresh or thawed baitfish, typically mullet or ballyhoo. A dredge made from imitation rubber baitfish. And finally, a dredge made from strips of plastic with holograms of fish. I use rubber ballyhoo dredges. I know anglers who use the other two with great results as well. It is extremely time consuming to make a natural dredge which is only good for one day of fishing. If you are interested in building your own natural dredge, use my recommendations for constructing a rubber ballyhoo dredge as a guide. If using mullet, keep in mind that a two-ounce egg sinker is required on each mullet to make them swim properly.

Construction of a rubber ballyhoo dredge takes up approximately one afternoon of your time. The reward more then outweighs the effort. Begin by purchasing a bar similar to the one in the illustration. This bar runs around $4. Multiple bars increase in cost depending on the size. The second step is to rig the rubber ballyhoo.

A 10-bait single-bar dredge.

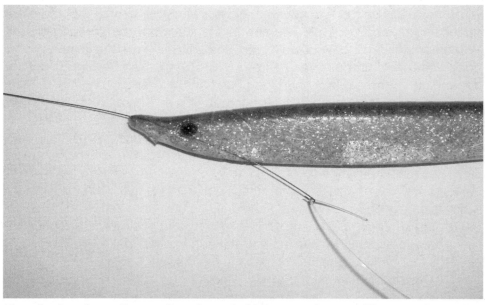

Bend a hook on the end and work 125-pound monofilament from the center of the nose down and out the first hook opening in the body of the ballyhoo.

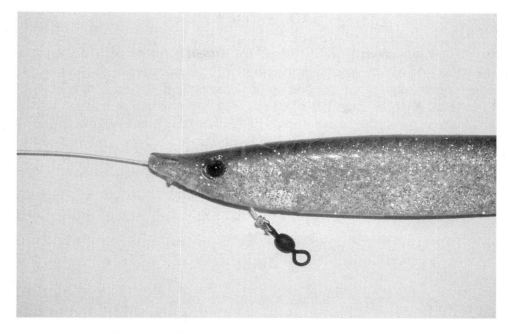

Tie a small swivel onto the end of the line.

Use a piece of number 12 wire. Bend a small hook on one end and work 125-pound monofilament from the center of the nose down and out the first hook opening in the body of the ballyhoo. Tie a small swivel to the line to prevent the ballyhoo from sliding off. Rig 10 in this manner, more if you want a larger dredge. Leave about 20" of line on each bally for rigging.

When rigging multiple ballyhoo inline, the ballyhoo need to have the leader threaded through the center of the body. This is accomplished by carefully pushing the number 12 wire through the whole ballyhoo, then coming out the center of the tail. Hook the leader and pull it up through the ballyhoo and tie off to the swivel. All ballyhoo leaders are crimped to a snap swivel for attachment to the bar. This prevents line twist when trolling. Leave four inches of leader for ballyhoo attached to the outside of the bar. Space the inner ballyhoo about 10" off the bar. This gives the appearance of a school of bait. A weight is required in front of the bar to keep it under water while trolling. Typically, a 24- to 32-ounce inline sinker handles the chore. I place the sinker four feet in front of the bar and rig on 400-pound monofilament. Imagination is all that is necessary to construct several dredges in different colors and sizes.

TROLLING SPEED

"How fast were you trolling?" It's a question that pops up anytime dejected anglers try to obtain information from successful anglers. However, conditions change depending on the wind, water current and state of the ocean. All three dictate boat speed. Finding out another angler's speed is a starting point, but speed should be decided by observing how the baits are working in the water. Trolling with the current requires boat speed to increase in order for the bait to swim properly. Just the opposite is true when running against the current. If rigged bait looks natural while being trolled, chances are the speed of the boat is correct. Of course, if fish are not cooperating, then changing boat speed is one alternative when trying to turn on a bite.

BIRDS

Anglers are not the only fishermen on the ocean. A look toward the sky reveals flying fishermen. Bird's survival depends on being good fishermen. Meaning, when they come down to the water's surface... we better

From its vantage point, the bird can see a lot farther than we can.

pay attention!

With our high-tech fishfinders, depth sounders, sonar graph recorders, radar, GPS, and VHFs, it's a wonder fish have a chance. But, empty fish boxes offer proof that anglers need all the help they can get offshore. Years are long gone since my boat's "equipment" comprised of only a compass and depth finder. However, with little to monitor back then, time was spent scanning the horizon for birds, breaking fish, and weed lines. Does technology have us glued to LCD screens when we should be looking elsewhere for fish?

Gulls, terns and pelican work the inshore waters, while further offshore, storm petrels, jaegers, shearwaters and gannets direct fishermen to the action. Keep all eyes scanning the horizon for the following indicators.

Five or more birds heading in the same direction should give you a new bearing to troll. Birds can see feeding action with their height advantage long before fishermen can notice birds on the horizon. Also, a bird's acute hearing tunes into action from great distances. The drone of engines overshadows the squawking of birds.

A flock of birds racked up is a floating giveaway. The feeding action has stopped on the surface. However, it may still be continuing underneath. The birds, patiently waiting for another outbreak on the surface, are drifting with the tide. That means you should troll against the current, to find the fish.

A hovering bird or birds are probably over deep baitfish. It is only a matter of time before larger fish begin to feed. Do not give up on an area that birds are watching.

Several storm petrels fluttering on the surface are likely feeding on oil droplets of baitfish recently slashed to pieces. Oil slicks may even be observed giving off an unmistakable odor.

When birds have directed you to breaking fish, troll the edges so the fish are not driven down. If casting, position the boat upwind and drift down into the action.

TEMPERATURE BREAKS

Pelagics and baitfish have little to draw their attention in the vastness of the ocean. Temperature breaks are something different in the environment which draw baitfish, and in turn draw feeding predators. A one-degree break may be all that is necessary to provide action, although a three- or four-degree break most often does. Troll parallel to the break on the cold side. No success, troll the warm side. Still nothing? Troll a zigzag pattern until fish are located.

WEEDLINES

Weedlines tend to form after a couple days of calm weather following storms. They are a fish haven. You name the species, and it can be found around weedlines. Dolphin are probably the most notorious resident taking cover in the shade, while waiting for the next meal. However, the baitfish seeking refuge in the weeds attract all pelagic species. Often weedlines are two or three miles in length, many times longer. Once located, weedlines should not be abandoned until worked thoroughly. I have never encountered a decent weedline that did not provide some kind of action. I am the first to tell you that fishing around weedlines is a pain in the #$%. The constant winding in and checking of bait to remove weeds can get on an angler's nerves. To help in this situation, tighten up the spread. This allows the bait to be observed when fouled by weeds and also allows you to get closer to the weeds without constant line entanglements.

Find flotsam mixed in the weeds, such as a board, and it is probably prudent to shut down trolling and switch over to bailing dolphin (chapter 10 under dolphin details this fishing technique) for some fast action. Finding a weedline without other boats is a fisherman's dream when offshore.

UNDERSTANDING THE THERMOCLINE

Time and time again through out this book I am going to refer to the thermocline. The fact is, it is extremely important when it comes to finding success when either trolling, live baiting or drift fishing. I am a certified dive master and have spent many hours studying fish around wrecks and under the ocean's surface. On my first ocean dive many years ago, I encountered the thermocline. Slowly descending the anchor line, I was suddenly hit in the face by a wall of cold water. I had been warned that this was going to occur, but was not ready for the slap in the face once I reached a depth of approximately 50'. The thermocline is a stratification of cold and warm water. It is more prevalent during summer months than winter, when layers of water tend to mix together. Why is this important? Because pelagic fish are temperature-sensitive. The water above the thermocline may be 78-degrees, below the thermocline it might only be 60. The water temperature is fairly consistent from the surface down to where the water stratifies. Then suddenly, there may be a 10- to 15-degree temperature change, at times even more.

Another important characteristic of a thermocline is the fact that it is often associated with a layer of cloudy, mucky water. This layer at times can take up 10' of the water column, where there is almost zero visibility.

My underwater experience has shown water clarity above the thermocline normally is not as clear as the water below, especially true after a period of calm weather. Then again, depending on the time of year, water clarity can remain the same from the surface to the bottom with little more than a slight temperature break at the thermocline.

Offshore anglers realize the importance of horizontal temperature breaks very quickly when trolling, because they attract fish and provide opportunity. The thermocline temperature break may not be as significant as those on the surface, still, they are important when examining the vertical water column.

In order to identify the thermocline, increase the gain on your depth finder. If sediment is suspended were the stratification occurs, it bounces back a signal making the thermocline identifiable. It is easy to see the importance of why understanding the thermocline helps you catch fish. In the following chapters, you will see how the identification is useful.

— CHAPTER SEVEN —
NON-TRADITIONAL TROLLING TECHNIQUES

There are times when normal trolling techniques fail to produce results. Anglers have two choices when this occurs: continue the present course of action, which is not catching fish, or try something different. My philosophy has always been the latter—try something different. Changing trolling speed, color, or type of bait is often all that is necessary. However, there are times when drastic measures may be required. The following ocean trolling methods may seem unorthodox, but many times are just the trick for putting fish in the box.

PLANERS

For years I used planers on the Chesapeake Bay while fishing for stripers, or rockfish as they are commonly referred to. I never really considered using a planer for ocean trolling because of the speed factor. I'm not sure who to give credit to for first using a planer in the ocean, but he or she was a wise angler. On days when tuna refuse to rise to the surface to feed, a planer is just the ticket for getting down to their comfort zone. It also places a bait in the wahoo's favorite territory. There are two ways to rig a planer for ocean trolling. However, before getting into that issue, it must be understood that trolling around six knots requires a good size planer if an angler expects to pull a bait at a depth of 30' or more. A size six or greater planer puts a lot of pull on a rod. A 50-class outfit can handle a planer up to size four. Anything larger and an 80-class outfit is required.

I am going to recommend a minimum distance of at least 50' between the planer and bait. This is a long way to wire a fish! Most experienced offshore fishermen place the bait 100' or more from the planer. It goes without saying this distance is too far to hand-wire a fish. There are two options. The first being a heavy class outfit, designated as the planer rod. The rod should have roller guides to ease winding crimps onto the reel. This rod is rigged with a planer that can be removed from the line while the fish is being fought. This may sound impractical, if not impossible, but believe it or not that is not the case. This setup allows the planer to be removed when coming within reach, while fishing line is reeled in. First step in setting up the outfit is to attach snap swivels to the planer. The swivels are used to attach the planer to the fishing line.

With the planer rigged, it is time to prepare the rod. Slide four crimps onto the fishing line and locate them about 100' from the end of the fishing line. Second step is to crimp two pieces of fishing line for the planer to be attached. Laying the planer next to the line, take a measurement from the ends of the snap swivel with the planer in the "tripped" (straight) position. Crimp one-inch pieces of line for the front and rear of the planer. This makes two loops where the snap swivels may be placed. You want the loops spaced so when the planer trips and the fish is fought, the stress is placed upon the fishing line and not the rear of the planer. In this fashion the planer is not under tension when it's time for removal. Use extreme caution when crimping the loops, do not damage the fishing line.

Just because a planer can be removed does not mean it is an easy task when a tuna or wahoo is exerting force on the end of the line, but after a while it becomes a matter of routine. The planer can be removed by one person if rigged properly, although two anglers make the task easier. One person gently pulls on the fishing line with gloved hands to obtain a little slack at which time the second person removes the planer from the line. The crimps wind right onto the reel and the fish is fought to the boat.

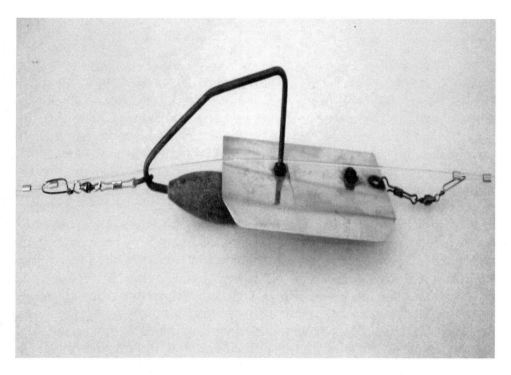

Planer in tripped mode, as it would be when fighting a fish.

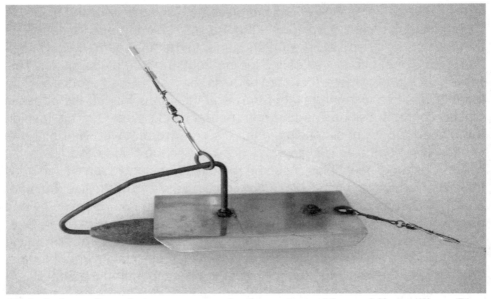

This is how the planer appears in the set position while trolling. The loose fishing line allows room for the planer to trip.

The second alternative is to run the planer on a separate line attached to the boat, similar to the theory of using downriggers. A release device may be attached to the end of the planer to attach the fishing line. But this requires the planer be pulled up each time there is a bite. A better option is to use a snap swivel with a rubber band. In order to use this rigging technique, begin by placing the bait 100' behind the boat. Now attach a rubber band to the fishing line snugly. The rubber band is then attached to the eye on a snap swivel. The snap swivel is clipped onto the planer line. As the fishing line is slowly let out, the swivel slides down to the planer, placing the bait at whatever depth the planer is set. Anglers can tell when the swivel comes to end of the planer line by the lack of tension on the fishing line. Place the rod in the holder and set the drag. When a fish strikes the bait the rubber band breaks, allowing you to fight the fish. To reset the system just use another snap swivel and rubber band. At the end of the day when the planer is removed from the water you will recover all your snaps. The disadvantage of this system over an in-line planer is that you are unable to adjust the depth of your bait quickly when reacting to the fish finder. However, I feel the trade off is more than worthwhile since 80 class tackle is not necessary for pulling the planer.

GO FLY A KITE

If memory serves me correctly, flying a kite as a child was not that easy. Too much or not enough wind, the tail not long enough, but mainly, lack of knowledge of how to keep the kite in the air was the problem. Take flying a kite on land and multiply it by a factor of around two and you will arrive at the difficulty of using a kite offshore. Then why do fishermen use them and put up with the hassle associated with kite fishing? That's easy: they work! Kites bring a whole new aspect to bait presentation. A live bait dangling vertically into the water or trolling a rigged bait skipping on the surface can only be accomplished by using a kite. Ideal for trolling or keeping live bait splashing around on the surface, kites open up other options to fishing. They are not going to be used every day or when fishing for every species, but the trouble associated with their use is more then worth the effort.

Fishing kites on the market today fly very well and do not require a tail like the kites we grew up with. Many are manufactured according to wind speed, however some are universal and fly in from four up to 20 mph of wind. Adjustment of the line where it attaches to the kite bridle allows for changing wind speed and the spars may be changed for wind conditions.

Kites open up a whole new world of bait presentation.

Follow the directions for the type of kite purchased for flying instructions. It is necessary to dedicate a rod for the purpose of flying the kite. A short rod equipped with a 4/0 reel is a good setup. 30-pound test line is adequate for this reel. One or more lines may be fished off a kite.

The kite rod is rigged in the following manner for use with one line. Insert a barrel swivel 75' from the end of the fishing line. A small type swivel is necessary since it must be wound onto the reel. A Spro or stainless steel Bill-Fisher Krok swivel works well. This is followed by an outrigger clip and a quality ball bearing swivel, attached to the end of the line. When deployed, the kite is let out 75' at which point the swivel catches the release. Attach the fishing line to the release clip and let the line out the desired distance from the boat.

For fishing two lines on a kite, two different size swivels are used. First step is to drill out the hole on an outrigger clip that allows the small swivel to pass through. Rig by inserting the larger of the two swivels 150' from the end of the line followed by the rigger clip that is drilled out. Insert the small swivel in the line 75' from the end, followed by the unaltered out-rigger clip. Attach a quality snap swivel to the end of the line. When in use, the first small swivel passes through the drilled out rigger clip but catches the unaltered clip. Once 150' of line comes off the reel, the larger swivel catches the drilled out clip to carry the second fishing line from the boat. This setup can be used to fish while anchored, drift fishing or trolling.

Clips customized for kite fishing with multiple lines.

The release clip on left in photo (clip closest to kite rod) has been pre-drilled with a hole large enough to allow the clip to slide over the small swivel. This swivel is 75' from the kite and passes through this first clip, however it will catch the second clip (right clip in photo) which will be used to carry the first fishing line away from the boat. A second larger swivel is tied at 150' and will catch the pre-drilled clip for a second fishing line.

TROLLING A KITE

Using a kite when trolling allows the bait to dance or skip on the water's surface—which at times is found irresistible by fish. A point that must be remembered when trolling a kite is there is no turning around. The kite is dictated by the wind not the boat. The boat may come off the wind up to 90 degrees, which places the kite at a 90-degree angle to the boat. However, any more then a 90-degree turn of the boat places boat movement in the direction of the wind. Meaning, the kite does not stay aloft. If trolling circles on a particular lump or edge is the plan for a day of fishing, leave the kite in storage. However, if most of your fishing can be worked against the wind, the kite is the ticket for the day.

When a large fish is hooked up that requires using the boat to assist in landing, it is prudent to wind the kite rod in first. This allows the boat to maneuver in any direction while fighting the fish.

There are two choices for setting the hook. When billfish are observed on a bait, the angler can snap the line from the clip with a sharp jerk; this allows a drop back. The other method, which I prefer, is to freespool with the line still in the rigger clip. Once the fish swims off and increases the rate of line disappearing from the reel, set the hook. This does not allow for a hard set, but I have found it is adequate for the initial strike and can be followed by a second setting of the hook when the line comes tight. Circle hooks and kites work well together, since all that is necessary to set the hook is winding the line after the bite.

Tuna find a bait jumping out of the water very enticing. By raising the rod tip up and down, the bait can be made to "fly" from the water. If tuna are observed on the fish finder, this procedure repeated a couple times every 30 seconds is a trick for putting tuna in the box. The tuna eat the bait just as it comes off the surface of the water. They may miss the bait several times, but just seeing tuna airborne is a thrill in itself. The kite gives the bait action that cannot be duplicated with outriggers.

Either rigged bait or artificial lures may be used for trolling off a kite. Stick with skip bait or surface type lures since the kite does not allow bait to run well under the water. The Carolina Yummee Fly-n-Fish are ideal for fishing with this method since it is the only way to make the flying fish lure appear natural. Try trolling the Yummy in the following fashion: Position the boat so the kite is off to one side of the boat and the Yummy is running in clean water. Turn the boat into the wind, then across wind. This quickly places the kite from one side of the boat to the opposite, which speeds up the bait, causing it to skip and fly across the surface. At times this drives tuna wild.

USE A KITE FOR LIVE BAIT

If you plan to sailfish with live bait, do not leave the boat slip without a kite. They are that effective. Kites are ideal for trolling, but they may even surpass this when using live bait. A live bait splashing and swimming around on the surface often is the ticket to a memorable day of offshore fishing. No leaders for fish to shy away from, just an enticing bait. The type of bait to use is limited only by what is available swimming in your neck of the woods. Mullet, goggle-eyes, blue runners, menhaden, pilchards, and cigar minnows all produce results. Rig these live baits by using a hook of an appropriate size. Bait can be hooked through the back or just above the eyes through the socket. Large bait may be bridled which is explained in chapter 5.

Live baits swim in circles when held by a kite. Due to this, a quality swivel must be used between the leader and line to prevent twisting. It is also beneficial to attach a piece of bright ribbon or marker where the swivel is located. Fishing line is almost impossible to see when 150' to 200' from the boat. The ribbon allows you to see how much leader is in the water and how deep your bait is swimming. I've recommended spacing baits at 75'. This distance works for me. You may want to tighten up the distance for bait presentation to give the appearance that bait is close together, but be careful to keep bait separated far enough to prevent creating a tangled mess.

— CHAPTER EIGHT —
CHUNKING FOR TUNA

Chunking for tuna is relatively new when a person takes into consideration how long recreational anglers have been going to sea and using different tactics for catching tuna. I was at a marina in Maryland, swapping stories at the watering hole one summer evening, watching charter boats come to the scale. Comments surrounding the decent catch (with a hint of jealousy) flew around the Tiki bar as an assortment of flags was observed being flown by most of the boats. One of the charter boats raised everyone's eyebrows and the amount of fishing chatter, when several decent yellowfin were thrown on the dock. As a newcomer to the charter fleet fishing out of the marina, the captain was still "out of the loop." Nonetheless, with very little fishing experience, he smoked everyone on this day. Fishing pride runs deep, so I did what any self respecting fisherman would: As one of his charter clients walked over to order a round in celebration, I congratulated him on the catch and asked the three questions: how, when and where.

Not being a seasoned fisherman, he gladly shared what he knew— caught tuna most of the day anchored somewhere in the ocean, on little fish. This story may not seem unusual or strange. However, this occurred in the late 70's, at a time when everyone mostly trolled for tuna. The rest, as we might say, is chunking history.

Every year the number of fishermen who chunk increases compared to those that troll. Even paying clients jump aboard charter boats expecting to chunk, decreasing their opportunity to catch other species. Be that as it may, charter clients want to catch tuna, and chunking is a method that produces fish.

Let us first focus on using butterfish for bait. These are readily available and the mainstay for those that chunk in the mid Atlantic region. They are available in frozen boxes called flats. Usually two to three flats suffice for a full day offshore. But, before walking out of a bait store, check the flats to make sure they have not been thawed and re-frozen. Fresh frozen butterfish have clear, clean eyes. More then once I have opened an inferior flat of bait. You will want to discover old bait before running all morning, so check the bait before going through the inlet!

Circle hooks will out-fish J-hooks two to one when chunking. The beauty of the circle hook is that tuna hook themselves with the rod in the holder. I prefer an 11/0 with a slightly offset shank. The offset can be put into the hook by using two pair of pliers to bend the eye in the opposite direction of the hook point.

To rig a butterfish go in the mouth with the hook, come out a gill, come under the fish, and reinsert through the gill on the other side. Completely embed the hook within the fish. Done properly, the butterfish will look natural with the leader coming out of the mouth. Butterfish spin in a moderate current when anchored. Keeping the mouth shut will reduce spinning. A piece of rigging wire run through the upper and lower lip and twisted shut is a quick and easy way to accomplish this. The tail can also be cut off to reduce spinning, or slice the fish in half with a diagonal cut. In a strong current it is often better to drift fish then anchor. This keeps the bait from spinning since it drifts along with the current, assuming the wind and current are running the same direction. Tuna are very reluctant to feed on a bait that spins.

It is difficult to deceive a tuna, especially yellowfin. Make sure the hook is completely concealed in the butterfish. Whether to use fluorocarbon as a leader is not even up for discussion. However, there is room to quibble over the leader poundage. Remember, fluorocarbon is not invisible. Bright sunny days with crystal clear water create conditions where tuna become leader shy as their vision is just about unbeatable. Start with the lightest leader you feel comfortable using. I begin with 50-pound test. When I visually watch tuna swim up to a bait behind the boat and not feed upon it, I drop down to 40, then 30. I've actually used 18-pound fluorocarbon in order to get yellowfin to pick up the bait. It is difficult to boat legal size tuna on that size leader, but if it is the only way to hook-up...

Bluefin normally are not as picky as yellowfin, especially when feeding deep. A standard chunking leader is a six-foot piece of fluorocarbon tied to a small black barrel swivel. Since a light leader cannot be wired by hand, it must be short enough to allow gaffing of the fish.

Cut each butterfish into five or six pieces and begin a chunk line by throwing a piece spaced about every six feet, with an occasional handful thrown in for good measure. It is a good idea to precut half a flat, because when the bite comes on there is little time for cutting up chunks.

A mistake I have observed: after a hook up, the chum line is stopped or broken during confusion in the pit. Everyone has a job, someone must continue to throw chunk to keep fish behind the boat. If the crew's ability allows multiple hook-ups, great! Other wise, fill the box one at a time. But, do not stop chunking or everyone on board will be watching the boat next to you catch your school of fish! It is not uncommon to be mixed in with 100 or more boats anchored up over a lump with only a handful catching fish. Do not lose your school of fish to someone else.

Another tactic is to always carry menhaden oil. Once fish are behind your boat, a couple drops of menhaden oil helps keep them in the vicinity. Fishfinder makes an IV-style drip bag ideal for dispensing menha-den oil, similar to an IV bag used in hospitals. It allows anglers to control the flow of oil to maintain a slick, and keep tuna in the area. Keep in mind that chunks or chum must also be used. The oil by itself is not sufficient to hold tuna. Another method to increase tuna activity around your boat is to use a bucket of frozen menhaden or mackerel chum. Cut a couple two-inch square holes in a five gallon bucket of frozen chum. This provides four or five hours of chum flow (depending on water temperature) which attracts all types of baitfish and pelagic species. Fish activity around a boat draws fish!

THE SETUP

The chunking setup consists of suspending baits at various depths that correspond with the chunk line. The chunk's rate of descent will vary day to day depending on the current. Lines consist of floaters (no weight) right behind the boat, to lines set at a depth of 100' or more with up to 20 or more ounces of lead. Suspend weighted lines under floats to maintain depth. Many anglers use balloons for floats, and simply tie the balloon around the fishing line to secure it in place. When the balloon is reeled to the rod tip, the fishing line slides through the rubber and you can continue retrieving it. Use egg sinkers for weight. Slide sinkers at least 20' up the line and hold in place with a rubber band. No bites, increase distance of the sinker to 100' from hook. Anywhere from one to six ounces of lead is nor-mally sufficient. However, occasionally there will be a strong current below the thermocline, making heavier weight necessary. A bait positioned five feet off the bottom can be the ticket for action, many days. Bluefin tend to feed deeper more often then yellowfin, but both may be caught right off the bottom, even in 30 or more fathoms of water. A bait suspended just above or just below the thermocline is also a great location.

HAND FEEDING

Finicky tuna may be coaxed into feeding by hand feeding the bait to them. This is accomplished by rigging a line with no weight, only a leader and circle hook. Use a piece of butterfish and be sure none of the hook is exposed. Throw in a handful of chunks along with the rigged piece. Set the drag so the line may be pulled off the reel by hand, but with enough tension to prevent backlash when a strike occurs. Strip line from the reel by hand and allow the baited piece to drift along with the handful of chunks. Once it has drifted out 100 yards, wind it back in and repeat. Many times tuna feed in the chunk line 50 or more yards behind the boat and refuse to eat a stationary piece of butterfish not drifting with the current, but they will strike a hand fed bait.

Using this method you will feel the tuna pick up the bait. At this point, there are two ways to set the hook. Allow the tuna to swim as the rod is removed from the rod holder, or push the drag up to the strike position before removing the rod from the holder. Either way works, but on occasion finicky tuna drop the bait when even a little pressure is felt from the drag, making it better to allow the circle hook to set from the rod holder.

If baits are being picked up and immediately dropped, the tuna are being sensitive to line resistance. Times like this call for free-spooling. Do not apply drag until the tuna swims off. Very light thumb pressure is required to prevent backlash until the drag is increased to set the hook.

CHUNKING TRICKS

Here are a couple additional tricks to try when the chunk bite is slow:

• Drift a line with a whole butterfish 30' from a float, with no weight. Allow it to drift out 200 yards from the boat before winding in and repeating.

• Set a line just above the thermocline with a whole butterfish and do the same thing, drifting the line 200 yards from the boat before repeating.

• Occasionally, especially if you are chunking too heavily, tuna eat way behind the boat and do not come to the bait. Slow up, by throwing a piece only when the previous piece goes out of sight.

• Fresh or live bait can open the door to successful fishing when butterfish are not on the tuna menu. Proficient with a cast net? Live spot or mullet make excellent baits when anchored up on a lump. They catch tuna, and just about anything else swimming in the ocean—I have taken several marlin on live spot when tuna fishing.

• Fill a five-gallon bucket with fresh small menhaden. Use them as you would butterfish. Menhaden are hard to beat when chunking. The scale's reflection of light is excellent in a chum line and tuna inhale them eagerly.

• Put an effort into catching live squid as bait and be the envy at the scales! Even thawed frozen squid work well mixed in when chunking. Many days the tuna prefer them over every other bait. Use squid whole, conceal the hook inside the body cavity and freespool it in the chunk line. Do not lock yourself into a rut of fishing the same way all the time.

Fish are opportunist, feeding on what is available. Staying flexible and willing to try something different increases catches. One summer while fishing off the Delmarva coastline, scallop boats from up North invaded the area. The scallop guts being discarded behind the boats from shucking scallops created a different type of chunking. Scallop guts became a choice bait and was obtainable from the trawlers working the lumps. Clams could be substituted and caught tuna when scallop guts were not available. However, that was the only year in my memory that this method of fishing produced such dramatic results.

Take along a flat of butterfish when running offshore for a day of tuna trolling. Even if trolling is the plan of attack, do not be left trolling around an anchored fleet if the chunk bite comes on. Always cooperate with other fishermen when anchoring and give ample space for fighting fish.

Finally, if the fleet is drifting.....drift! A fleet of 50 boats drifting should tell arriving anglers one thing—drift fishing is how fish are being caught. Besides, if you decide to anchor in the middle of a drifting fleet, you will be in the way of all the drifting boats. Do so at your own peril and do not be surprised to find out that your mother was not married to your father.

— CHAPTER NINE —
BASICS OF BATTLING TROPHY FISH

"The big one always gets away!" Well, maybe not all the time, but there must be a reason for the saying. Every fisherman has at least one experience where a trophy fish somehow managed to become a great story. Are all trophy fish destined to get away? It seems bad luck is blamed more often then not, when actually, terminal tackle, drag setting or any one of a thousand reasons could be the culprit. Let us examine what causes the pendulum to swing to the fish's side of winning a tug of war.

Over my years of watching novice and experienced anglers alike doing battle, there are what we might call "routine" mistakes. By familiarizing yourself with these costly mistakes, you may not end up becoming an expert at losing trophy fish.

JUST A LITTLE MORE PRESSURE

This is the number one mistake I have observed over the years. It is executed when trying to slow down a fish taking line or when adding just a smidgen of extra pressure to bring a fish within gaffing range. Fishermen must have some type of genetic brain defect that says, "When a fish is taking line, increase the drag!" 30-pound test mono is not going to hold up to a 50-pound yellowfin screaming line when an angler places a thumb on the spool, nor will an 80-pound outfit with 500-pounds of blue marlin on the end. The thumb move accomplishes two things: a lost fish and a blister. Allow the reel's drag to do its job. Preset drags at 20- to 25-percent of the line strength and leave them alone! Use a scale and set the drag at a straight pull off the reel as discussed previously. Just to get a feel for pressure, raise the rod and take a second reading with friction from a bent rod. Depending on the rod length, guides etc., the pressure may increase to 40 or 50 percent of the line's rating.

Not sure how much pressure is transferred with a slight touch of the thumb? Tie the line to a fixed object. Hold the rod at a 45-degree angle with the drag set and start backing up quickly, simulating a fish taking line. Now apply thumb pressure. The line snapping is a great indicator of how little pressure is necessary to exceed the breaking point. Combine thumb pressure, excitement, and line disappearing from a reel, and well, you get the point. Experienced anglers can get away with increasing or decreasing the drag. However, if you are using a quality reel, once the drag is set it may be prudent to take your chances with that setting.

A fish that stretches out 400 yards of line increases the line tension from water resistance. Fight the fish with the rod held no higher then a 45-degree angle to reduce pressure. Backing off the drag a couple pounds is not out of the question. Nor is backing off a drag when the fish is at boat side with very little line out, since there is little line stretch to relieve pressure if the fish runs. But, unless the angler has a good feel for the amount of pressure being exerted, it is difficult to reset a drag under tension. After using the same set of Penn International outfits the past eight years, I'm able to tell by the bend in a rod the amount of pressure being applied by the angler, and can adjust drags accordingly. Keep in mind I watched these rods every day to gain this knowledge.

Gaffing is another pressure-sensitive area. Wiremen develop a feel for how much pressure can be exerted using a certain pound test leader when wiring a fish to the gaff. If you think maximum pressure is being applied, and the fish decides to increase pressure from the other end, the leader must be released. Work the fish back in and begin round two, three or however many attempts it takes until the fish can be brought to the gaff. Remember, if double line is used and the drag is increased once the double line comes onto the spool (one of the reasons to use a long double line,) if the fish runs, the drag must be backed off.

MULTI-FISH

This is a situation we all want to experience every fishing trip. They are what dreams are made of, but also can be an angler's nightmare and a difficult encounter to overcome. This is a recipe for disaster: mix a triple hookup of 60-pound tuna, screaming lines crossing each other, and three excited anglers, and the outcome normally equals lost fish and definitive statements. Mono has very little tolerance to heat generated by friction from crossed lines. Crossed lines leave only seconds to act before young ears need to be covered.

As difficult as it may be, cut a line. This is no time to debate which line has the largest fish or which angler should get to fight their fish because it was hooked up first. If lines are crossed and cannot be immediately undone, reach out and cut a line and hope to untangle the remaining lines and salvage one or two fish. If you are the person cutting lines, you will probably be educated by your buddies. Fishermen with lines cut have informed me that my mother was not married before my birth and that I have K-9 blood. Nonetheless, it is how I handle crossed lines and attempt to save fish. Cannot bring it upon yourself to cut a line? Then at least back off drags and point the rods at the fish until lines can (hopefully) be untangled.

UNDER THE BOAT

An angler's natural reaction is to raise the rod when fighting a fish. However, when a fish sounds under the boat and the rod is raised high, the line rubs on the chine of the hull and creates friction—although, not for very long! When fish sound, the rod needs to be pointed down toward the fish. It may even be necessary to hold an angler's belt while he bends over to get the rod down in the water to prevent the line from rubbing or entangling on the strut or prop. Fight fish under the boat by winding down to the water, lifting the rod to a 90-degree angle and winding back down. Not by lifting the rod overhead, then winding down.

TANGLED LINES

The laws of physics govern the breaking strength of line. If the line gets wrapped around the anchor rope, lower unit, trim tabs, transducers, or anything else, loosen the drag to reduce pressure and friction. This may allow the fish to swim the line out or at least give a shot at trying to unwrap the line. Odds are certainly against the angler in these situations. However, Lady Luck just may be tired of hearing your barrage of words and smile upon you.

NOON RULE

The "noon" rule, or 90-degree rule, refers to the position of the rod. Anglers fighting fish where line is stretched out behind the boat should not raise the rod past the 11 o'clock position, which creates more then a 90-degree angle with the line. The same rule applies with fish sound under the boat. Do not raise the rod to where more then a 90-degree angle develops. The increase in drag pressure is astonishing when the rod is raised above the head when a fish sounds under the boat. This move often results in line separation.

SLACK LINE

Wind! Wind! Wind! If I only had a dollar for every time I have found it necessary to say that to an angler. The reasons anglers stop winding vary from becoming caught up in watching the fish put on an aerobatic display to the angler saying, "I'm too tired." If there is one sure way to lose a trophy fish, it's to stop winding. Always keep a taut line and a bend in the rod. If you let the line go slack, the fish can shake the hook out of its mouth. This is especially true with billfish.

Another way slack occurs is when the angler pumps a big fish to gain line. The angler drops the rod faster then the line is being cranked in. Or, worst yet, lifts the rod only to lower it before reeling! The proper method of pumping consists of raising the rod slowly, and retrieving line with the reel as the rod is lowered. If the drag gives line to the fish when the rod is raised, the angler is raising the rod too quickly. Pumping or working a fish is done as a fluid motion, not by quickly jerking the rod up and down.

STEADY PRESSURE

Keeping steady pressure on a fish wins the tug of war. The fish is in a battle for its life and is giving all it can to escape. You, the angler, on the other hand, are only driven by the desire to accomplish catching a trophy fish. Many anglers work so hard in the first 10 or 15 minutes of the battle that they become winded and are unable to accomplish the task at hand. Steady pressure wears a fish down. How long this takes naturally depends on the size of the fish and amount of pressure being applied.

A 200-pound tuna on a 20 class outfit puts the angler's ability to the ultimate test. This situation requires the maximum amount of pressure that can be exerted by the equipment in order to wear the fish down. On the other hand, the same fish on 50 class equipment, although not a cakewalk by any means, is within the grasp of most anglers. Murphy's Law dictates the largest fish always bites on the smallest line. When this occurs, keep in mind steady pressure and this saying: "You rest... the fish rests!" Anglers cannot relax a couple minutes to take a breather, because the fish (particularly tuna) take the lull in pressure to recoup energy, placing the angler at a disadvantage and back in a new fight.

Once the hook is solid in the fish there is no reason to reset the hook. Violent jerks from your end of the line only send the vibrations to the fish, and sometimes cause erratic or ballistic behavior, not to mention placing unnecessary strain on knots and swivels. Additional jerks also can enlarge the hole in the fish's mouth where the hook penetrated, increasing the chance for the hook to be thrown. Treat a trophy fish as you would a woman: use finesse, be smooth and gentle. Trying to use brute force to overpower a fish seldom wins the battle.

DON'T COUNT YOUR CHICKENS

"I can't wait to sink my teeth into sushi..." The tuna battle is just beginning and the angler is already getting ready to break out the teriyaki sauce. This tells me full attention is not being applied to the task at hand, which is concentrating on catching the fish. Anglers should not become overconfident and believe that the battle is won from the onset. It demands all the angler's attention, and no mental mistakes (which lead to physical errors). As the saying goes, "It's not over until the fat lady sings." These couple examples are typical: Wire in hand, gaffs just waiting to be sunk deep into the fish. The angler relaxes, thinking the end is in hand. The fish surges with a second wind, the wire man releases the leader for fear of breaking the fish off. The rod is jerked out of the angler's hand and is saved only by being attached to the harness. The loud sound, however, is that of the line snapping.

As bad as that scenario is, it can be worse. Captain Josh Ruskey, who at the time was running the *"Size Matters"* tells of the following incident during a shark tournament:

"A mako had eaten a whole bluefish being fished live off of a kite. The green 300-pound mako came to the boat in five minutes. No one was keeping an eye on the angler, who, believing the mako's demise was at hand, unsnapped the reel from his harness and was holding the rod in one hand while he watched the mate wire the fish. When the mate could not hold the leader any longer and had to release it... well, an 80 class Penn International looks very pretty glimmering in the water on its way to the bottom!"

Never assume the battle is over. Bragging rights do not exist until the fish is aboard. Anglers need to always be prepared for the unexpected!

COACHING

"Lower your rod tip. Listen, lower your rod tip! LOWER YOUR ROD TIP!" Somehow, fighting a fish makes some anglers deaf or they become so focused on the battle they shut everyone and everything out. There should be a person on board whose job it is to coach the angler during the battle. Helpful directions spoken into the angler's ear can prevent the disaster of losing a fish. The coach monitors the cockpit, boat movement, amount of line out and most importantly, line build-up on the spool which is often overlooked in the excitement surrounding a large fish. The coach needs to speak, not yell or shout, directions. It is the angler's responsibility to listen to the coach.

Out of the corner of my eye I can see the bend in the rod is being lost. Turning around I notice that the angler has not only stopped winding, but does not have a hand on the reel and is trying to adjust the belt, which had slipped to the side. I look up just as the white marlin jumps and sends the lure flying through the air. Was it the angler's fault? No, it was the coach's. It is not the angler's job to adjust the belt or harness. This is another job the coach must perform, while the angler is concentrating on the fight.

FIGHTING CHAIR VS. STAND-UP

If you own a pocket sportfishermen the question is moot. However, not having enough space for a permanent fighting chair does not mean anglers must stand when locked into a two hour battle with an ornery pelagic. Few anglers can endure a battle of that magnitude without sitting down, and sitting with a gimbal belt does not work, because the rod rides too high and is uncomfortable. A few options, regardless of the size of boat, allow anglers to sit and fight fish.

The first and most common method is to attach a gimbal as an accessory to a portable boat chair or on a seat already mounted in the boat. Another option is a rod holder which fits under the lid of a cooler. This allows the angler to use the cooler as a chair and fight the fish while sitting on top.

A fighting chair is a great equalizer when the tuna weighs as much as you. Author's wife, Marie, works a 100-plus-pound bluefin.

Side jump seats which have rod holders can also be installed and are a great option. These fold down out of the way when not in use, but in seconds provide a solid seat for fighting fish. Every boat, even if equipped with a chair, needs to carry harnesses and belts for those days when multiple hook-ups are encountered—which brings us to fighting fish from the stand-up position.

First, remember to adjust the harness and belt before the fish strikes. Many fish are lost while trying to adjust the equipment and attention is diverted from the battle. Stand-up belts should be worn over that area where we all like to have fun, not high around the waist. A harness should be adjusted so the arms are not responsible for holding the weight or pull of the rod. If adjusted correctly, pressure against the tip of the rod is transferred to the back so the arms may relax. Legs slightly bent and a straight back is a comfortable position for fighting the fish. In addition, the angler has a better feel for the rod and pressure that he or she does when the rod butt is secured in a gimbal on a fighting chair.

Stand-up requires the angler to follow the fish around the cockpit. Standing as if your shoes are nailed to the deck in one corner is the first step to disaster. Most anglers that do not want to move are afraid of being pulled over the gunwale. I have found that a hand grasping the top of the

Even with a chair available, many anglers would rather stand up to fight fish.

harness gives confidence to move around the boat. Follow that fish!

USING THE BOAT

Two schools of thought exist concerning the usage of a boat when fighting a fish. One is to work the fish from a stationary boat and let the fish tire itself out. The problem with this method is all the line that gets stretched out. This increases the chance of cut-offs by other boats, fish, or debris. It is true the fish is doing all the work, but that same can be said for the second option, to use a moving boat (which is what I prefer). The less line out, the better I feel chances are the catch will be successful. Chasing or following a fish to keep it close to the boat does not mean less pressure. Decent pressure can still be applied by lifting the rod and retrieving line even as a boat moves towards a fish. It does take coordination between the angler and captain to assure slack never has a chance to occur, but the reward out-weights the effort. If using stand-up gear, the boat may be run at a 15- or 20-degree angle toward the fish in order to retrieve line. Just make sure the angler keeps winding and the rod maintains its bend, keeping pressure on the fish. Backing down on a fish is great if you are fishing off a battlewagon. However, smaller self-bailing boats will find chasing the fish to retrieve line more comfortable and safer then backing down with waves washing over the transom or splashing over the engine well.

SAFETY HARNESS

A safety harness should be considered when pursuing large pelagics. More than once has someone lost their life by being pulled over the side of a boat when either wiring or gaffing a fish. Regardless of how strong you are or how much experience you have in a pit, the danger of entanglement in leaders capable of taking a fisherman off his feet, or just an accident where balance is lost, can make anyone a victim in the water. Commercial models are available starting around $75 and should be given serious consideration, especially when fishing for large pelagic species such as blue marlin or sharks.

— CHAPTER TEN —
TARGETED SPECIES

ATLANTIC BONITO

Scientific name, Sarda sarda, this fish is commonly referred to as bonito, or common bonito. This member of the tuna family is typically overlooked, while its larger cousins get all the attention. The name bonito is often used in confusion when identifying the false albacore or skipjack tuna, which are two different species. Mention you caught a bonito and many anglers turn their nose up, when actually the fish provides pleasant table fare.

Typically found all along the Atlantic seaboard from inshore waters out to the 20 fathom line and beyond, the fish seldom exceeds four or five pounds. Often caught on heavy tackle when pursuing other species, it is often thought of as a nuisance. However, when targeted on light tackle this small tuna can more then hold its own and provide a lot of enjoyment.

Once inshore waters hit the mid 60's, the fish invade inshore lumps and shoals, occasionally even feeding close to shore. They can be distin-

Richard Reagan displays a Bonito taken while fly fishing with Capt. John McMurray. Photo courtesy of One More Cast Charters, Inc.

guished from the skipjack tuna and false albacore since it is the only member of the tuna family with longitudinal stripes on its back. The skipjack tuna also has longitudinal stripes, however, they are located on the stomach. Another sure way to tell the difference is the prominent teeth of the bonito, which are used to grasps its prey (compared to other species of tuna which have their teeth recessed and gulp in food when feeding).

Catching bonito is easy: troll for them using small spoons or lures. They also find rigged bait appetizing, but the offering should be kept on the small side. Small ballyhoo rigged on 5/0 hooks are a good choice and also increases your chances of taking other species that may be feeding in the same area.

Planers used to troll small spoons just off the transom are deadly on bonito. Sea Striker and L.B. Huntington both make a size number two planer, which is ideal for this use. Set the planer down around eight or 10' using 25' of leader for the spoon. The planer will be visible, as well as the spoon flashing under the prop wash. But, bonito are typical tuna in that they find feeding close to the transom no problem.

At times these small tuna school up and feed on the surface. Spinning tackle equipped with 12- to 15-pound test line is more then sufficient to tame the fish. However, do not be surprised if the first run covers 50 or more yards as the hooked bonito tries to regroup with the school.

When chunking for yellowfin or bluefin tuna, bonito may be observed cutting in and out of the chunk line. It is times like these to break out the light tackle and use very small chunks of bait to take the fish. Do not assume larger pieces of bait will take larger fish; they sometimes pass by large pieces of bait, preferring small offerings.

Bonito make up part of the daily catch when targeting larger species. As I mentioned before, they are not known for their culinary pleasure, but it only takes one dinner to prevent anglers from releasing this small member of the tuna family when in pursuit of other species. If you find yourself fishing on one of those days when the ocean seems devoid of life, down-size a couple of your baits and see if bonito can make their presence known to break up the monotony of a slow day offshore, and put some meat in the box.

DOLPHIN (MAHI-MAHI)

Coryphaena hippurus, mahi-mahi, dorado or dolphin, call it what you choose. But pound for pound, this is the underrated lightweight champion at the end of the line. The names may not sound appealing, but, this fish baked with lemon pepper leaves a clean plate and makes many an-

Bull dolphin such as this are true trophy fish.

glers wonder why they do not target the species more often. I cannot recall any angler ever referring to them by their given names, Coryphaena hippurus or Coryphaena equisetis. But, depending on what region of the Atlantic you fish, mention mahi mahi, dorado or dolphin, and everyone lends an ear to catch what is being said. No wonder, it only takes one encounter with a 40-pound bull (male) dolphin, with line-burning runs and an aerial display that rivals white marlin, to acquire the fever for catching these fish.

Identifying the sex of this fish is very easy. The male has a blunt forehead, as if it rammed into something. The female on the other hand has a typical round fish shape to the head. Mahi-mahi migrate north following waters temperatures as they climb into the 70's.

Coryphaena hippurus is the common dolphin. Coryphaena equisetis is the lesser known pompano dolphin. (Neither to be mistaken for the mammal dolphin!) The two varieties are difficult to visually tell apart. However, hippurus is very abundant and the most often caught, while rare pompano dolphin have a rounder body shape. Nature has given these fish the ability to reproduce at eight inches of length, which is obtained at about four or five months of age. Their ferocious appetite allows rapid growth, achieving a length of 45" when two years of age, with a life span of about four years. Extremely plentiful, excellent table fair and one of the most beautiful fish that swims the ocean, dolphin are a prized game fish. And, if that is not enough for you, they are not picky eaters and devour just about anything that comes in their path. Now, that's the perfect sport fish!

Dolphin are often caught mixed in with the daily take while trolling offshore. But, serious anglers in pursuit of dolphin look for them under Sargasso weed or any type of floating debris. Lobster balls along the 100-fathom line in the northeast are a popular gathering place and can normally be counted on to provide action. It is here that dolphin search for their favorite meal, flying fish, which make up 25-percent of their diet. Shallower inshore waters find smaller fish up to three or four pounds. It is common for schools to move over inshore shoals and occasionally provide an unexpected catch for bottom fishermen. Floats attached to sea bass pots even hold small schools hovering underneath sometimes. However, most fish will be caught in the deep by one of two methods: trolling or bailing.

Trolling is the way to throw large dolphin in the fish box. Fish over 20 pounds (called "gaffers") tend to be loners or travel in pairs swimming in search of meals. Smaller fish (called "chickens") up to about 20 pounds stay schooled up around anything floating. Occasionally larger fish will be mixed in with these. However, trolling is the way to produce the wall-hanger that

The author's wife with a "gaffer" dolphin she caught "bailing" on spinning tackle.

can push the scale to 50 pounds or better. Numerous times I have taken a large bull and female simultaneously while trolling. Peanut dolphin (small dolphin less then 12") can be a downright nuisance, attacking and stripping natural baits. Fish tend to school according to size, so move on in search of larger fish when pestered by peanuts. Unless, that is, you want to increase your chances of catching marlin. When small dolphin are abundant, keep a sharp eye on the spread for marlin—which find them irresistible. Upping your bait size and using multi colored lures and skirts over rigged bait to represent dolphin increases your chances of raising a marlin.

What to drag behind the boat for dolphin does not seem to make a big difference, as long as the bait size is around the size of flying fish (six to eight inches). Preference to color may lean toward the blue hues and brightly colored lures/skirts. However, color does not seem to be of utmost importance. When a dolphin is hooked, maintain boat speed leaving all the baits in the water. This creates multiple hook ups with most, if not all, of the rods going down. If trolling a weed line, or if lucky enough to find the dolphin's favorite haunt, a pallet, pull the bait or lures within 10 yards. This normally produces strikes if fish are present.

Once fish are located trolling, you may want to switch over and bail dolphin. This method consists of using light tackle and casting bait or lures to the fish. Dedicated dolphin fishermen forgo trolling and strictly search out weed lines and floating structure until a school is found to bail. There are a few tricks, which if followed will provide many tasty meals.

• Keep several types of bait available when bailing dolphin. Ballyhoo, squid, bonito, skipjack or false albacore (save one or two instead of throwing them back when trolling) will do nicely.

• Precut bait into pieces. No one will want to take the time to cut bait when the action gets hot and heavy.

• If the action slows and fish get finicky with one bait, change to a different offering. Artificial lures can be cast with success. However, I find cut bait to be more productive.

• Dolphin can be slow starters, rushing out from under cover to look at the bait only to return to the shade. If the fish are shy taking the hook, throw a small handful of bait to get them feeding.

• Once a dolphin is hooked, keep the fish in the water until a second is hooked up. Do not land the first fish until another has been hooked. A school will not leave the area when a hooked fish is left in the water. I cannot over emphasize this point, ALWAYS KEEP ONE HOOKED DOLPHIN IN THE WATER. If all the hooked fish are brought onboard, you may find yourself looking for another school.

• Keep a couple spare rods rigged and ready to go. Teeth are going to cause cutoffs, and crossed lines are a sure thing. The last thing you want to do during a feeding frenzy is tie on a hook with fumbling fingers with your buddy shouting in your ear to hurry up, all the while watching a 10-pound dolphin swim in circles! There are times when dolphin are not particular and wire line could possibly be used, but do not waste your time. Use fluorocarbon leaders and retie hooks when cut off.

• Keep the line tight when these notorious scrappers try to throw the hook. Dolphin catch air and perform somersaults in a show that always brings cheers of excitement. Never one to give up, be prepared as they jump right at the transom, during landing. The angler must be ready to point the rod or take up slack.

• To prevent the fish from becoming airborne next to the boat, hold the leader down close to the water when wiring. This is especially true when they are caught trolling with the boat maintaining motion. If utilizing wind-on leaders, when the fish is close to the boat, hold the rod tip near the water. When dolphin feel a sharp angle on the leader they follow it right to the surface.

• Dolphin are not very thick throughout their body length. This presents a problem when a gaffer is being landed. If you use a large gaff, the fish turns slightly and slips out of the hook. Use a two- or three-inch head gaff on large fish; the slimmer hook simplifies the gaffing procedure and assures landings.

Once you put these tricks to use and catch some fish, remember that dolphin are dazzling fish and they reflect a wide range of brilliant colors, but if you want to capture the beauty of your catch on film do so when the fish is first brought onboard. Coloration quickly fades to a plain white/silvery once out of the water.

This is one fish where we must think conservation. Dolphin are prolific reproducers, with females dropping 80,000 up to 1,000,000 eggs three times a year. Their numbers are in no danger at the present time. However, it is possible to catch whole schools of fish when bailing dolphin. Have a blast, but only take what you need. Practice catch and release. It is easy to get caught up in the excitement and without realizing it, the cooler is soon full of fish that are not going to be consumed.

It is not uncommon for dolphin to miss strikes on rigged bait. This is probably due to dolphin having the ability to grab a bait, instead of inhaling it as some species do. When missed strikes occur, drop the line back followed by a couple jerks, then wind quickly, to entice a second strike. This should be standard procedure for missed bites. Those "mystery" bites, which often come from dolphin or marlin, require a drop back to bring the fish back on the bait. Artificial lures only require jerking forward to entice a second strike.

My grandfather, like most fishermen, had his own philosophy on how to catch fish. He took every opportunity to instill in me his favorite saying, "Big bait equals big fish!" As a child sitting on the end of his pier fishing for perch, he would insist that I use the largest bull minnows. At the time, little did I know this was due to the fact that he did not feel like cleaning small fish. Nonetheless, my catches were large in size but not numbers. Quality over quantity. This line of thinking was true when it came to fishing for perch in the creek and certainly applies when fishing for dolphin in the

**Pop Cooke and Tom Kessler take a
moment for a quick photo while bailing gaffers.**

ocean. When pestered by those small peanuts that just love to tear into a spread and ruin every rigged bait, up your bait size to deter the attacks.

Fish flopping around on the deck going crazy is not a situation that anglers find entertaining. Okay, the sound of a beating tail does bring a smile to the face, as does blood in the pit! However, it bruises the flesh of the fish and distracts from the flavor. Not to mention damage that may be sustained by a person or equipment. You have heard the saying "if it was not for bad luck I would have none at all"?

To illustrate the point: a large bull dolphin was thrown onto the cockpit deck, about this time the angler let go of the rod, which fell across the fish. One quick flip of the tail and... splash! Re-spooling the 450 yards of line that was removed while retrieving the rod off the bottom was cheap, compared to having the reel taken apart and cleaned after its bath. Solve this problem by placing fish in the kill box. Most of the time the hook removes itself. If not, use a wet towel to cover the eyes of large fish. The towel calms them down before they beat the boat and you to pieces.

FALSE ALBACORE

Scientific name — Euthynnus Alletteratus, commonly known as fat albert, albie or little tunny, which all refer to the torpedo-shaped fast swimming false albacore. The word albacore, normally associated with great tasting tuna, whether it be canned or fresh, unfortunately does not apply to this fish carrying the name. Worthless (as far as I'm concerned) for the dinner table, the fish does make for a great adversary. Fly fishermen prize the fish for its power and speed, but often find it too much to handle on a fly rod. When caught on appropriate tackle one may call this a gamefish. However, caught offshore trolling for other species it is mostly referred to as a pain in the @%#. Typically 10 to 15 pounds, the fish is mistakenly caught by anglers after taking a trolled line intended for yellow or bluefin tuna. Capable of making a great first run, the fish has fooled more then one angler into thinking they are hooked up to a fish larger then they are.

Often referred to as a bonito, the two should not be confused since this species offers no use other then for bait when bailing dolphin or fishing for shark. The fish can be identified from a bonito or skipjack by the spots between the pectoral and pelvic fin on the front of the belly. The fish also has irregular or broken stripes above the lateral line. This is in contrast to the straight lines on the bonito or skipjack. False albacore favor coastal waters but may be found offshore as well. The fish can be seen schooled up breaking water while chasing small baitfish. When this is observed casting lures simulating minnows brings hookups, to challenge any angler's ability

As a catch and release fish, false albacore certainly brings a smile to the face, as Paula clearly demonstrates.

to land fish on light tackle. Once hooked, be prepared for the fish to perform blistering runs, quick turns and even double back and swimming directly at you, making it all but impossible to retrieve line quick enough to keep it tight.

KING MACKEREL

I think of this species more as an inshore fish then offshore. However, since they often frequent the 20 fathom line and are encountered when trolling for other species, I have included them in this book. King Mackerel, named Scomberomorus cavalla, are one of the fastest swimming predators you will fight. Large fish are nicknamed "smokers," and not without good reason. This name refers to what they are capable of doing to a reel. Kings, or kingfish, as they are commonly called, are pelagic fish that normally congregate or school around shoals. However, large fish tend to be individuals and often feed by themselves. Experiencing kings attacking a bait can be thrilling if the fish skyrockets during the process. They have the ability to come out of the water flying 15' or more, then crash down on their prey with extraordinary accuracy.

Fishermen along the Carolina coasts make this fish a prize catch,

**Tom Kessler displays a king caught
trolling drones along the 20 fathom line.**

which is clear with all the tournaments held each year in its honor. Florida fishermen also find this species a sought after target. However, as you move north from the Carolinas the excitement of catching kings wanes. Off the Delmarva coast, which is near the northern end of the kingfish's range, the fish are not targeted by many charters or recreational anglers. Although, some summers, depending on migration patterns, abundant amounts of fish can be found on lumps out to the 20 fathom line. I find the fish a welcome addition for summer charters when fishing out of Ocean City, Maryland. Half-day charters are limited to fish selection since prime fishing areas require long 50 to 60 mile runs. Summers when kings make a showing offer our inshore charters the opportunity for more then bluefish, false albacore, bonito and an occasional bluefin.

Trolling accounts for its fare share of catching this species, but live bait is without a doubt the number one way to hook up large kings. Slow trolling or live baiting by utilizing a kite or float to suspend baits all take large kings, so long as one uses wire leader to prevent cut-offs by these toothy fish. Kingfish are not picky eaters, but using indigenous baitfish to the area returns the best results. Pinfish, mullet, ballyhoo, herring, spot, bluefish, the list goes on and on. My personal favorite up north is menhaden, which are found just about everywhere along the inshore waters of the Atlantic with the exception of south Florida. Fishing from the Carolinas south I use pinfish when available. Menhaden schools are visible when the water is flat calm, if not, let the pelicans direct you to the bait. Their keen eyes pick out the schools of baitfish from above which results in their dive-bombing display, revealing the location of the baitfish. Easily caught with a cast net, menhaden offer a big target which is the key to catching big kings.

All anglers want to catch the big one! Use the theory "big bait equals big fish" to reduce the amount of smaller kings that grab your line, and target in on large smoker kings. In addition, larger menhaden slow-troll better then smaller ones, since they are stronger and capable of swimming longer. Nonetheless, whether you have small or large bait, be careful not to drown the bait by pulling them through the water. Slow troll only at a speed which keeps the lines straight. Slow trolling actually allows the fish to swim, not get dragged, through the water.

If fishing on a shoal, edge or area where kings are known to frequent, it may be wise to drift live bait suspended under floats. Kings prefer the warm water above the thermocline, so keep baits on the shallow side. The same live bait rig used for slow trolling may be used when drifting. If

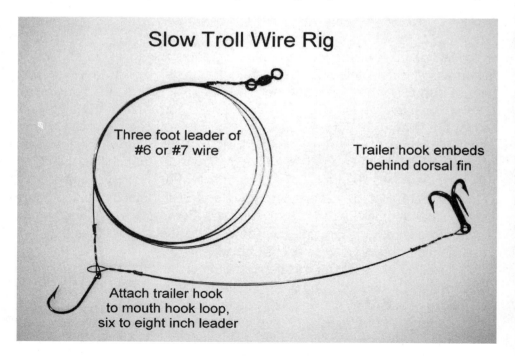

Slow Troll Wire Rig

Three foot leader of #6 or #7 wire

Trailer hook embeds behind dorsal fin

Attach trailer hook to mouth hook loop, six to eight inch leader

Rigging live baitfish requires this simply-constructed rig.

using a kite, place one or two baits in a position where they swim on the surface, creating fish-attracting activity. Increased movement of the baitfish is a telltale sign that a predator is close by and should tip anglers off that a strike is not long in coming. When pods of baitfish are migrating close to shore in the fall, try slow trolling just off the beach for those kings looking for an easy meal.

Targeting kings when trolling for other species is simple. Planers are effective when used in conjunction with artificial lures. Trolling spoons up to seven or eight knots are preferred. One of my favorite lures for Kings is a number 3-½ drone used with a number two planer. I have used Clark spoons with great success, however, I find the drone accounts for more fish. Another reason I prefer the 3-½ drone is that bluefin find them very desirable. It is not uncommon to catch bluefin around shoals when water is over 100' deep. Occasionally a king cuts off a spoon, but seldom does it take it deep in the mouth, so I do not recommend using a piece of wire leader—which reduces the action of the spoon. However, if a wire leader is desired, use a single strand piece of number four Malin hard wire. This is 40 pound test wire with a diameter of only .013. The trade off with this wire, compared to the flexibility of stranded wire, is that it's not very visible. Use a three-foot piece of wire with an 80 pound test swivel to make the connection to the monofilament.

Kings have no problem coming to the transom to take lures. Use a 30' section of 80 to 100 pound test leader. Locate the planer off the transom down around 10'. This places the planer and flashes of the spoon within your sight under the white water. Set the strike drag with only enough tension to prevent it from slipping from the pull of the planer. Kings make a good first run and if a smoker decides to take the lure a tight drag may cost you a fish and tackle. When baitfish are observed on the depthfinder running at a depth of 20' to 30', up-size the planer to a number three. Set your rig to run the spoon at the baitfish's depth. A spoon runs higher in the water column then the planer. Keep in mind when setting the planer that a 30' leader with a spoon may be four or five feet shallower then the planer. So set the planer accordingly. Running spoons deeper in the middle of the day when the sun is high also brings results, on days when kings are shy coming to the surface.

Kings will also take cedar plugs run on flatlines, along with rigged ballyhoo if kept to the smaller side. Most kings caught trolling are going to be school fish, so keep the offering small.

BILLFISHING FOR MARLIN

Before getting into the meat of the subject concerning how to catch marlin, let us quickly examine the current state of affairs surrounding the fishery. Another formal review on the status of white marlin was completed in 2006. The final outcome boiled down to a couple of changes for the recreational fishermen. First, it will be allowable to harvest 250 blue and white marlin during tournaments. Once this number is reached, tournaments are required to be catch and release only. Second, only circle hooks will be allowed in conjunction with rigged natural baits in tournament situations. These measures, while questioned by many anglers, at least allow for a recreational fishery. Back in 2001, a petition was submitted to have white marlin come under the Endangered Species Act and sought to stop long lining in areas of U.S. waters during spawning and feeding periods. The status review conducted during 2002 found it was not warranted to list white marlin as endangered at that time. However, it did find that the measures being taken by the International Commission for the Conservation of Atlantic Tunas (ICCAT) were not sufficient to prevent over fishing. The ICCAT is an international organization to which the U.S. belongs, which

If this sight behind the boat does not excite an angler, check his pulse!

keeps watch over billfish along with other pelagic species. They report marlin numbers have declined year after year. Why a decline? Marlin are caught as a by-catch from the international long line fishery targeting tuna and swordfish. ICCAT has determined that white marlin are being killed at a rate eight times faster then they can replenish themselves.

The United States leads the way in billfish conservation. U.S. commercial fishermen are required to release all hooked marlin and most recreational anglers voluntarily release marlin unless they are being brought to a scale in a tournament. Still, in the year 2000, the U.S. was responsible for 42 metric tons of white marlin landings—an astounding number, considering the figure only represents four percent of the total Atlantic catch. How do recreational fishermen fit into the dilemma? Sportfishing represents one tenth of one percent of the number of white marlin killed. Even so, it appears sport fishing may suffer the consequences of over fishing from the commercial end. Let us hope that ICCAT and commercial fishery arrive at a solution that reduces the killing of marlin, thus allowing their numbers to increase, providing recreational billfishing for generations to come.

Now, with regards to catching marlin, regardless of the type of billfish being pursued, there are some basics that can be applied to each species. This section covers catching procedures that applies to white or blue marlin. Both species are covered individually under their own separate chapters, but the following suggestions apply to both fish.

Paying attention to the spread is crucial if you hope to achieve success when billfishing. However, anglers cannot watch the spread 100 percent of the time. This opens the door for Murphy's law—when you turn your head is usually when the fish bites! Let's assume the bite on an artificial lure being pulled off a short rigger is not observed. The sound of the clip releasing draws your attention. At this point, the lure falls freely and momentarily slows or stops. The fish has not been seen, however, the first step is to immediately pick the rod up and look for the fish. The marlin may come back on the lure and pick it up. If so, immediately set the hook hard and do not give the fish time to spit the bait.

If the marlin does not immediately pick up the lure, wind up the slack and put movement back into the lure. The fish probably has submerged at this point and is not in sight, however, this does not mean it is not considering coming back on the bait once movement of the lure begins again. Keep eyes scanning all the baits, because if the fish does not come back on the first lure it may attack a different one in the spread.

Take the same situation with a natural bait. The first move is not to pick up the reel, but to immediately place it in freespool, allowing the bait to slowly sink. The billfish, after smacking the bait with the bill (which caused the clip to release) is expecting the bait to be stunned. It should now turn and pick up the "stunned" baitfish as it sinks.

You should get the idea by now that you must know what offering is being pulled on each line, since those with baits and those with lures each require a different response when hit. And you should also realize by now that you always need to be prepared to jump into action when billfishing.

Even when paying attention to the spread and seeing a billfish come up behind a bait, you will not have a lot of time to decide what course of action to take. The decision of taking the rod in hand or leaving it in the holder needs to be made. With lures, it may be prudent to begin winding away from the fish while the rod is in the holder. If the rod is in hand, raise the tip slightly and pull the lure away. As the fish attacks the bait he will open his mouth. Lower the rod tip, actually placing the lure in his mouth. When pressure is felt, set the hook hard. Many anglers prefer several hard short jerks when pressure is felt. I like two strong settings of the hook. Do not give the fish time to spit the lure. The setting of the hook is immediate upon feeling pressure.

The selection of lures that are used for blue or white marlin is overwhelming. Which are the best to use? The answer to that question may be found in your wallet. Tournament winning lures do not come cheap. Manufacturers such as Marlin Magic, Joeyee, Black Bart or Pakula begin around $50 a lure and may exceed $100. Sevenstrand even makes a "Sonic" lure which carries a battery and emits the sound of a distressed mackerel. (I never knew mackerel made a distressed sound!) However, at $200 a lure, I do not foresee one in my spread, nor could I find any other fisherman who has tried one to give me first-hand knowledge. Although the concept of an electronic acoustic lure does sound intriguing, before one graces my spread at that price I will need a proven track record. Of course, as the saying goes, "you only have to sell the lure to the fishermen, not the fish!"

Trolling natural bait for billfish seems to be a technique falling by the wayside with all the popularity surrounding artificial lures. Of course, naturals still probably account for the majority of white marlin hook-ups. One reason anglers may shy away from natural bait is the fact that some skill is required in order to catch fish. Acquiring drop-back skills can only be accomplished by actually having the opportunity to perform the move time and time again, until proficiency is obtained. Since all anglers learn the process beginning with their first billfish bite on a natural bait, the only preparation you can make is to be mentally prepared and know the steps of dropping back a bait beforehand.

First and foremost, as previously mentioned, and worth mentioning again, your chances of catching a billfish are greatly enhanced if the fish is observed before it attacks the bait. Eyes constantly watching a spread are imperative for successful billfishing.

Imagine a beautiful clear blue sky, one- to two-foot swells rising and falling in front of a light south-east breeze. You are working a two-degree temperature break along the west wall of a canyon. Several shearwaters display command of the air by gliding with wing tips barely off the water. A flock of storm petrels demonstrate their water dance while picking at the remains of baitfish floating on the surface. You inhale deeply to savor the aroma of fish oil that drifts off the water. The atmosphere has a "fishy" feeling about it. Anticipation mounts as each bait is visually checked and re-checked. The previous nonstop jabbering of the crew has turned to silence, and all eyes are fixed on the task of watching the spread. Your attention is drawn to the port short rigger where a submerged ballyhoo is emitting a smoking stream of bubbles. It flies out of the water for a heart-stopping moment, only to reenter with its enticing movement. False alarm. Piercing down into the clear blue water you start asking yourself questions. "Is that a fish? Is it a shadow? Am I seeing things? I could have swore I saw something...POP!"

The starboard flat line's gone off! If you must think what the next step is, chalk up another missed opportunity. Trolling for marlin with natural bait calls for action, not thinking. The process needs to be instinctive. As I previously stated, this knack is developed through experience, and there is no time to ponder what the next move is when a marlin presents itself. Rule number one: A game plan needs to be thought out and explained to the crew before lines are set. Be in the pit near the rods watching the baits at all times. You can be asleep and manage to hook up tuna or dolphin when the drag sounds off, but a marlin is not that forgiving.

Visual confirmation of what's happening with the bait dictates your move. If I do not see the marlin before the strike and the clip releases, I hit freespool and drop back as I lift the rod out of the holder. In conjunction with this move, the thumb on the hand controlling the reel must apply slight pressure to prevent backlashing. By dropping the bait back from the rod holder a split second is saved, which can be the difference in a pick-up or a swim-away. The marlin expects the bait to be stunned once struck with the bill. If not, a second attack may occur, but I have found many times that marlin discards that bait in favor of another. If the bait is not picked up after the drop back, wind using several short jerks, then free spool a second time, even if the fish cannot be observed. Note: when a reel is placed in freespool, point the rod at the fish. This allows the line to fall without friction from the rod guides and allows a better feel with the thumb, which is applying only enough pressure to prevent a backlash.

Often a strike occurs when you turn to speak with someone or look at a different bait. When a rod is hit and missed, do something! It amazes me that someone standing next to a rod says, "he missed it" without picking the rod up when a bite occurs and does not come tight. Drop the bait back immediately and try to sense a pickup by the marlin. One indicator that the marlin picked up the bait can be observed by watching the line come off the reel. The rate of line peeling off the reel increases after being picked up by a fish which is swimming away with the bait in its mouth. However, before this, the first indicator can be felt by the thumb maintaining light pressure on the spool.

Hopefully, of course, you'll have your eyes peeled and will see the billfish come into the spread. In this case you should be able to identify if the fish is a white or a blue, and react accordingly. Since each marlin requires a slightly different reaction, baiting them when you know what species is attacking will be covered shortly, in the sections on each specific fish.

For either type of marlin, there is probably no greater thrill then to use the bait and switch method to catch a billfish. Using a teaser to raise a marlin then switching a rigged bait for the hook-up is exciting, to say the least. It is a productive way to catch sailfish, whites and blues as well. The bait and switch allows an angler to become actively involved in the bite. Not that there is not enough to do when a marlin comes into a spread, but the bait and switch tactic is probably the ultimate for the sportfishing enthusiast. Just seeing a hungry marlin inhaling your bait 20' off the transom after being enticed from a teaser is worth the effort of trying this fish-catching method.

As in all types of billfishing, it takes practice and then more practice until the procedure becomes second nature. The method takes the coordination of two anglers, one to handle the teaser and another to work the rod. The first step excites the marlin and creates a situation where it becomes aggressive. This is accomplished by pulling the teaser away as the fish attacks. During this time, the angler with the rod prepares and gets into position so the bait may be thrown in or switched with the teaser. Once ready, the angler controlling the teaser jerks it away. This move must be quick and the teaser must be removed from the water or at least thrown several feet from the marlin. At the same time the bait is thrown in front of the marlin, who, now stimulated into a feeding mood, becomes very aggressive and switches over to the bait. It is imperative that the bait swim correctly when it hits the water. A spinning bait ruins the opportunity. The pitch bait should be rigged and tested before actual use.

Where to store a pitch bait can present a problem. The rod and bait need to be in the pit and ready for action. Many anglers dedicate a small cooler at the transom to hold the bait. Others secure a PVC tube with the bottom capped off, on the transom. This is filled with seawater and the bait is place inside, ready for action. Regardless of what type of system you come up with to hold the pitch bait, it must be immediately accessible when a marlin rises to the teaser.

BLUE MARLIN

Makaira nigricans...the big dog, the king. Actually we should say the queen, since females take center stage and grow in excess of 1000 pounds with males only topping out around 300 pounds. Arguably this is one of the most sought after pelagic species in the world, and is deserving of the title, "World's Premier Big Game Fish." From legendary story book fiction to factual encounters, regardless of what anglers have read or heard about this species, they are not disappointed when experiencing the catch whether it is their first blue marlin or the hundredth. Each and every experience with the largest of all billfish becomes etched into the mind.

These mammoths of the sea are common all along the eastern sea-

The author prepares to revive a blue marlin—a dream catch for most anglers.

board. A small blue marlin can sometimes be confused with a large white marlin to the novice billfisherman. The best way to tell the difference is the anal and dorsal fins. If they are pointy it is a blue marlin, as whites have rounded fins. There are fishermen that target these beasts and routinely hook up, pushing tackle and human endurance to their limit. However, for the average offshore angler, the trolling spread is set with an invitation to a mixture of species. When you fish the deep with a spread targeted at white marlin, dolphin or tuna, but want to increase your percentage of hooking the ultimate premier sport fish, consider the following instead of counting on inadvertent encounters.

The power and stamina of blue marlin demands heavy tackle. So put the 30's away if you plan to target blue marlin, light tackle just does not have the ability to put enough pressure on this fish. I have heard anglers bragging about catching 400-pound blues on 30 class outfits, only to mumble under their breath that the fish was totally exhausted and probably did not survive. This is not prudent sportsmanship and should be avoided at all cost. A successful catch occurs when the fish lives to fight another day. 50 class should be a minimum for tackling and having hopes of defeating this fish, with 80's or 130's preferred. Just the fact that some anglers rig and troll up 30-pound yellowfin as bait tells an angler what they are in store for. It is a massive undertaking to target these fish on a regular basis. Luckily for the average offshore angler, they have an opportunity to encounter these magnificent fish when trolling a mixed spread. If you have not experienced the thrill of catching a blue marlin, chances can be enhanced with only a few changes in a typical trolling spread. Keep in mind the big bait-big fish theory. This may not be true for all species, but fishermen only have to analyze the Marlin Project, taken from 1995 to 2000 at the University of Rio de Janeiro, Brazil, to draw a conclusion. The research examined the stomach contents of 69 blue marlin that were brought to the scale at tournaments, and revealed the following breakdown of their diet:

Tuna	64 percent
Mackerel	16 percent
Dolphin	10 percent
Triggerfish	5 percent
Flying Fish	5 percent

When one considers that the bulk of a blue marlin's diet comes from members of the tuna family, it takes a lot of guess work out of what size bait to use! Does this mean smaller bait will not produce? Absolutely not. My largest blue (over 600 pounds) came on a blue/silver eye-catcher skirted over a medium ballyhoo in a mixed spread. Many other captains I know catch blues on spreads set for white marlin or tuna. Then again, there are captains who believe in big bait. To what lengths will some anglers go to catch a marlin? As an example; after seeing a blue come into his spread, Captain Brain Porter on the *Enticer* reached into the kill box, rigged a 35 pound yellowfin, and caught the fish! (Currently, Capt. Porter is co-captain of the *Marli,* fishing out of Ocean City, Maryland).

There is controversy over which is the best rigged bait or whether artificial lures take preference over rigged bait. Ask five captains and mates who make a living charter fishing and you are likely to receive 10 different answers. Keep in mind, they are all correct since it is what works for them.

Rigged bait or artificial lures trolled in or very near the canyons is standard operating procedures. I have raised blue marlin inside the 30 fathom line and even heard of one caught in 10 fathoms. Nonetheless, this is a fish that likes a lot of water under it, so work the tip of the canyons out into the deep (50 fathoms and beyond) to maximize chances for success. While blues may tolerate water as cool as 68- or 69-degrees, warmer water in the upper 70's to low 80's certainly increase chances for encounters. Weed lines, temperature breaks and an ocean brimming with life is a winning combination for trying to raise a blue into the spread.

Whether trolling artificials or rigged bait, this fish often targets in on the larger baits in the spread. To increase your chances of tangling with a blue when offshore, dedicate two lines, a short rigger and flat line. Marlin are not intimidated by the boats or prop wash. By dedicating a short rigger and flat line, the bait may be observed during the strike to increase chances of hook-ups. Using larger offerings on these lines, such as horse ballyhoo, mullet, mackerel, or large artificial lures, ups the percentage of having a blue attracted to those individual lines.

Create activity behind the transom using large teasers, such as bowling pin chains, to help raise fish into the spread. Actually, the boat's white water is one of the best fish attractors. Many boats that have a track record of raising marlin have their resale value increased by literally thousands of dollars. It could be hull vibration, props, or some other factor, but some boats just raise more fish then others. If your boat is in this category, thank your lucky stars and do not change a thing!

On a charter boat I worked years ago, we had props that definitely attracted marlin. So many in fact, that we removed the props to prevent damage and only used them in tournament situations.

One trick if fishing on a boat with outboards is to slightly raise the engines to turn a lot of white water, in order to get a blues attention. Teasers and daisy chains carry the bulk of this responsibility, but the boat's white water helps. If using rigged natural bait, try using dredges to increase the odds of raising these big dogs. A dredge used in conjunction with a large teaser creates the illusion of predators feeding on baitfish. Locate the teaser about five feet behind the dredge for maximum results.

Blue marlin are not stacked up on every rip or edge. Many miles of ocean may need to be covered in order to raise a blue. If anglers are serious about upping the chances of catching a blue, high speed lures trolled at eight to 10 knots allows a lot of ground to be covered. Lures may be rigged in several ways. The first method is a stiff hook rig, and can be rigged two different ways. A stiff hook rig is made so the hook is prevented from freely swinging. One or two hooks can be rigged as a stiff hook. Let's begin with the single hook rig. Use multi-strand wire cable in 250- or 480-pound test, crimp an appropriate size hook for the lure being used to one end. Typically this is going to be a 11/0 to 13/0 hook. A piece of shrink wrap tubing is used over the crimp connection and the shank of the hook, to prevent the hook from moving on the leader. In a pinch, electrical tape can be wrapped around the connection for the same effect. Position the hook at the desirable location in the lure's skirt and use a crimp as a stop to prevent the lure from sliding down onto the hook. Hook position is a debatable topic and certainly a matter of personnel preference. I prefer the bottom on the hook shank to be even with the end of the skirt of the lure, believing its concealment is to my advantage. I am probably in the minority. Many if not most of the professional tournament fishermen I am familiar with fish for blue marlin with a rig where the hook protrudes past the skirt. This assists in hook-ups with short strikes and eliminates the fear of the skirt affecting the penetration of the hook. Those in favor of this rigging say that while trolling at eight or more knots, the hook cannot be seen in the turbulence made by the lure. While this is probably true, I still prefer the hook recessed within the skirt. Your rigging choice and decision is based upon what you are comfortable pulling behind the boat.

Not to complicate the issue, but another decision must be made when making a stiff rig. Is a one- or two-hook stiff rig better? Once again, two schools of thought prevail. While a two-hook rig increases hook-up percentage, it causes problems while trying to remove the hooks from large fish for release. In addition, two hooks in a fish's mouth certainly cause more damage then just one. Now, with my personal objections of two hooks set aside, let me say a two-hook stiff rig is your best shot at hooking up a blue marlin and the only way I would go if fishing in a tournament situation. Many anglers construct the rig by placing two hooks at a 90-degree angle to each other, while others favor 180 degrees, with the hooks facing away from each other. The last choice is zero degrees, where both hooks face the same direction. I prefer the 90-degree rig. This photo of a Pakula lure is rigged on a stiff rig with a 90-degree hook setting.

To make a double stiff hook rig, crimp a six inch length of multi-strand cable to one of the hooks. Use a crimp to make a small loop at the other end of the wire. Take another hook and align the eye of the second hook with the loop made on the wire of the first hook. Shrink-wrap the two hooks together at a 90- or 180-degrees to each other. Now attach the leader to the hook eye and wire loop by means of a crimp. Position the lure on the leader and use a crimp to adjust hooks to the desired riding position. Wire or mono leader may be used. I prefer abrasion-resistant, hard mono in 350-pound test. The lure can also be rigged on 49-strand stainless 250-pound cable.

It is important to keep an artificial lure moving when a marlin comes up on it at fast trolling speeds. They may become very aggressive and bat the lure around, at which point you do not want the flat line or rigger clip to release. By setting the clips tight, the fish can actually hook itself. Eight to 10 pounds of clip pressure assures a good hookup. Of course it is dif-

This lure was responsible for allowing the crew of the *Size Matters* to walk away with first place and $680,000 at the Big Rock Tournament in 2005, with a 529 pound blue.

ficult to set a clip at that precise poundage. To make this a simple matter, tighten the clips down and use a #32 rubber band to attach the line to the clip. Besides having around a nine-pound breaking point, the rubber band prevents the line from getting flat spots from a lot of clip tension. Be patient when a marlin becomes aggressive and attacks the lure. Pick the rod up and wait for the rubber band to break. The reel drag should be set on a strike setting of around 10 pounds. When the clip or rubber band releases, the fish is normally hooked. As the first run is made, slowly push the drag up and settle down for the battle which lies ahead. Many times the fish will be hooked outside the mouth. This is where a double-hook stiff rig has a large advantage over a single and why it is your best bet for hooking up a blue. Regardless of which manner you rig your lures, or which type of hook setup is on purchased pre-rigged lures, the setting of the hook remains the same when trolling fast.

Hooking a blue on a rigged natural bait is not rocket science, but it's not a walk in the park either. If paying attention to the spread, the marlin normally can be seen following the intended meal. Each fish is different, some may follow 30 seconds or more before striking, others attack almost immediately. Some may switch back and forth from bait to bait looking over each before deciding which to attack, or as occurs in some cases they may just swim away!

Patience needs to be a virtue practiced when the fish is first observed. If the marlin has not attacked, take the rod in hand. Movement which makes the bait imitate an escape attempt can be applied to provoke an attack. When the bill of the marlin strikes the bait, pull the bait slightly forward. This should stimulate another violent attack, at which time the reel should be placed in free spool—allowing the bait to appear stunned. The marlin will turn and pick up the bait; at this point the line leaving the reel increases dramatically. If the bait is on the small side, such as a medium ballyhoo, the hook can be set almost immediately. This is also the case if the bait is skirted with a lure or large lead head skirt, to prevent the fish from spitting it out. If the natural bait is of large size, allow the fish to run and swallow the bait before setting the hook. Anywhere from three to 10 seconds may be necessary before setting the hook hard, judged as necessary according to the bait size and fish size.

These recommendations are based on natural baits rigged with J-hooks. If you are intending to fish in a tournament for blue marlin, it is now required that a circle hook be used with a natural bait. The procedure for setting the hook is different then a J hook. Once the bite occurs, give the required time for the bait to be taken into the mouth. A natural bait rigged with a circle always has the hook at the front of the bait, meaning more time may be required before the following step. The setting of the hook is accomplished by pushing the drag into strike position from free spooling. This allows the line to come tight from the forward movement of the boat. Once the weight of the fish is felt, wind the reel. DO NOT jerk the rod, only wind the reel to keep the line tight. The fish is hooked! The hook-up cannot be improved upon by jerking the rod or trying to set the hook.

WHITE MARLIN

White marlin or Tetrapturus albidus if you prefer to use the scientific name, are found throughout the east coast region and may be encountered anytime the water is above 70-degrees and fishing in 30 or more fathoms of water. Although catches are occasionally made in 20 fathoms or less, 50 fathoms out into the deep is your best bet for catching what many anglers believe is the most difficult fish to hook. Their size is no comparison to the blue marlin, but they more then make up for the lack of size in their finicky

A tight line is necessary when a white comes out of the water, to prevent the hook from being thrown.

feeding methods. If you are serious about catching a white, Ocean City, Maryland, known as the "White Marlin Capital of the World" is a good place to start your quest. The Washington, Poormans and Baltimore canyons are favorite haunts for these pointy nose predators. Fishing off Cape Hatteras is another good choice to tangle with this acrobat of the sea.

The white marlin is my favorite pelagic to chase around in the Atlantic. Most anglers targeting white marlin are in agreement, they may very possibly have the most difficult mouth to penetrate with a hook. The boney upper and lower jaws leave little room for error. White marlin are the cause that I, along with many other fishermen, need to wear hats—because there is very little hair left from all the head-scratching!

Using finicky as a definition for their feeding habits may not be the best word to describe this sought after species. One day they commit suicide, the next only window-shopping the baits while you jump around the cockpit going from rod to rod. To say they are a difficult fish to hook on a regular basis is an understatement. Unlike many other species, the white marlin does not require heavy gear. With an average weight of around 50-pounds, 30 class outfits are more then sufficient for subduing these

Author (left) with white marlin caught by angler Ronnie Cooke on a Green Machine.

magnificent aerialists. Many anglers drop down to 20 class outfits to experience all these fish have to offer. Jumps and grayhounding runs while trying to throw the hook quickly puts a hurting on their endurance, and one can expect the fight to be similar to that of the sailfish.

But before catching a white, they need to be attracted to your spread. The typical teasers dragged behind boats for decades to raise billfish now have an added companion. The savvy modern angler has a dredge behind the boat in conjunction with a teaser to raise marlin. The dredge is filled with holograms that look like baitfish on plastic strips, or are made up with 15 or more rubber ballyhoo. Some dedicated white marlin anglers even take the time to rig dredges with natural bait consisting of ballyhoo or mullet, and swear the effort is worthwhile. While I do not put that much time into building a natural dredge each day, I never billfish without pulling a dredge made of rubber Bullyhoo. Chapter 6 covers these in detail. Can you catch marlin without using teasers or dredge? Absolutely, since we never know what is going to attack a bait—but their use is going to increase chances of raising fish greatly.

Before discussing what baits to pull, it may be helpful to understand the white marlin's food habits. As with many pelagic species, there is really very little known about the habits of the fish. They appear to be sight-oriented feeders and feed mostly during daylight hours. Temperature breaks often bring many fish into one area, although they are not thought to be a school fish. But, it is not uncommon to see several working together balling bait. The bill appears to be used to stun or kill their prey by slashing. However, based on stomach content, many times when feeding it appears they simply inhale the bait without slashing. Apparently, white marlin often overtake their prey by speed, rather than injuring it first. I have witnessed on many occasions a white come up on a bait and simply grab it and try to swim off, qualifying the theory that they do not always use their bill when feeding. If you are in a situation where the white just grabs a bait, remove all pressure from the bait by free spooling. Give time for the white to swallow the bait. Never less then five seconds, assuming it is a natural rigged bait. If you have a mixed spread out and are pulling rigged naturals off the long riggers or way behind the boat from the shotgun position, you may notice the rod slowly bending and the outrigger receiving pressure on the release clip. Often, this pressure comes from a white that has grabbed the bait in its mouth without slashing with the bill. Your first thought may be that the line has picked up grass or floating debris. When this occurs, again, drop the bait back, give it time, then try setting the hook. Why a marlin does not always slash the bait is a mystery, but mouthing a bait does occur often.

Stomach content shows marlin feed on squid, small dolphin, mackerel, flying fish and bonito. Keep in mind a white's mouth is not very big. Large baits probably account for more missed marlin then any other culprit, so keep baits on the small side when targeting whites. Trolling natural bait for white marlin is the number one way to achieve success. Unlike the blue marlin that may inhale a bait, whites need more time to maneuver a bait in the mouth before swallowing. Which baits to use? Ballyhoo without a doubt are the number one rigged bait pulled for whites marlin. Small, or "dinks" as they are commonly referred to, are easy for the fish to swallow and for you to rig. Mullet, normally rigged split-tail style, are another good choice. Squid is probably the white's first choice when it comes to the dinner menu. However, many anglers do not pull squid due to the hassle in rigging. In the rigging section there is a method I use which simplifies the rigging process.

Enticing a white to bite a natural bait is at the top of my list when it comes to excitement in life. Until you've experience the rush, it is hard to explain. I can only assume it is like a drug habit—once you do it, you cannot get enough! The fish normally shows itself before deciding to eat in the spread. Since it is imperative to see the bite in order to best react, trolling spreads targeted at whites are normally run tight behind the boat unless there is extremely calm water, in which case the baits may be more spread out.

When a white comes up on a bait and just follows, a few jerks on the line to makes the bait appear to be trying to escape may incite an attack. After the bait is slashed with the bill, place the reel in freespool and point the rod at the fish to lessen resistance of the line coming off the reel. Use only enough thumb pressure to prevent a backlash. Once you feel the white pick up the bait, there are a couple of ways to attempt setting the hook. I say "attempt" to set the hook, because no angler is going to hook up every marlin that presents an opportunity. Actually, if anglers new to marlin fishing can obtain a batting average of .500, they are on track to be a first rate marlin fisherman.

As mentioned, white marlin have a relatively small mouth and do not immediately try to swallow the bait attacked, unless it is a very small bait. Many times, the fish holds the bait in the mouth as it swims. If the hook is set at this point, chances of a hook-up are very slim. It is far better to give the marlin time to maneuver the bait into its mouth before swallowing. One way to achieve this is by waiting a period of time before setting the hook. This is probably the best alternative for those beginning to fish for marlin. Once the pick-up is detected, count to a minimum of three, preferably five, before setting the hook. I know anglers who give eight to 10 seconds of free spooling before setting the hook. This gives the marlin time to begin swallowing the bait. Another method is to watch the line peel off the reel after the pick-up. A marlin often slows up to swallow the bait, so once the rate of line leaving the reel is observed to slightly decrease, the hook is set.

These two methods only apply to natural rigged bait or a rigged natural without a skirt containing a lead head or some type of metal rigged on a J hook. In a case where a lure is used to skirt a rigged natural, such as a llander skirted over a ballyhoo, the marlin feels the awkward hardness of the lure in the mouth and spits the bait if given too much time. In situations where a natural bait is skirted, count to no more then three and set the hook. Knowing which bait is in what position behind the boat is crucial for knowing how to set up on a white.

Rigging with circle hooks requires a different method for the setting of the hook. Actually, there is no setting of the hook, only winding the reel after allowing the fish time to swallow the bait. Trying to set a circle hook only results is missed fish. If a natural bait is not picked up with either a J or circle hook, wind while giving the bait a couple short jerks, then free spool a second time even if the fish cannot be felt or observed. Many time the fish will come back on the bait and give you a second chance.

Remember: knowing what kind of bait is in which position of your spread is crucial for knowing how to set the hook. There is no time when a bite occurs to try and remember what type of bait is on the rod! Murphy's Law states that anglers are not going to be paying attention when a marlin comes into the spread. When I am caught flat-footed to a white marlin already on a natural bait, I hit free spool and drop the bait back before lifting the rod out of the holder. Acting on the bite before removing the rod from the holder can save fractions of a precious second. Finally, if a rod is hit and does not come tight, assume it was a marlin and free spool, do not stand in the pit staring at each other and say, "We had a bite, didn't we?"

Although white marlin do not have a large mouth, they still have no problem attacking larger artificial lures. Ten-inch to 12-inch lures are not out of the question. Select lures that create a disturbance in the water. Concave heads which smoke (create bubbles) or lures that generate movement when being trolled are good choices. Color does not appear as important as movement to churn up the water, however, bright colors on sunny afternoons seems to produce successful results. If hooking up a white on a natural is considered difficult, accomplishing the feat on an artificial is almost like doing the impossible. Of course, it is not impossible, but learning the technique is no easy task. I recommend pulling artificial lures from the short rigger position, where the lure can be observed clearly. When a marlin becomes interested in an artificial and follows the bait, take the rod in hand and raise the rod tip, pulling the lure away as the fish attacks the bait. He will become aggressive, very aggressive, and this is the situation you want to create. When the fish attacks again with its mouth open, lower the rod tip, allowing it to grab the lure. The fish will turn, and it is at this point that you try to set the hook. Do not give time for the fish to spit the lure. Once pressure is felt, set the hook with two or three sharp jerks.

The best advice I can offer when a bite occurs is to try and remain calm. I know this is much easier said then done when the crew is shouting at the top of their lungs while a white attacks a bait and the rod is in your hand. But, the bite may only last a few seconds and anglers must act quickly and calmly. Concentration and remaining calm will get the job done. Run over the process of hooking a white marlin time and time again in your head, it will prepare you for the actual situation.

Regardless of what type of billfish you find success with, I am going to recommend taking photos of your catch in the water. With that being said, you may notice that this book contains photos of whites being held in the cockpit. My charter clients who catch marlin want photos, as do many anglers fishing from their own boat. Smaller marlin, which I feel can be handled with wet gloves without doing serious harm, I bring aboard for a 30-second photo shoot. The fish is then carefully placed into the water, after which, the bill is held while the boat is placed in forward. This forces water over the fish's gills, and helps to revive it. The marlin will let you know when it has the energy to swim off, normally by jerking the bill from your hand. Whether the fish is brought aboard or left in the water, marlin are fighting for their life and at times totally exhaust themselves. Always revive your catch before watching it swim away to fight another day. To reduce internal damage, consider using circle hooks. More advanced rigging techniques for circle and J hooks are shown in the rigging chapter.

Why all the fuss about circle hooks? Dr. John Graves of the Virginia Institute of Marine Science completed a two year study on the survival rate of recreationally caught and released white marlin. Satellite archival tags were attached to 20 marlin caught on straight shank J hooks and 20 marlin caught on circle hooks. The study revealed seven of the 20 caught on J hooks died, compared to no mortalities of fish caught by circle hooks.

PRO TIPS

There are a lot of "experts" when it comes to offshore fishing. Some faces are easily recognizable because of television shows, other have name recognition due to their outstanding reputation. Then there are those who are relatively unknown except for their reputation and ability among their peers, other professional captains and mates. I am fortunate, in that I have had the opportunity to fish with some of the best offshore anglers, period. Capt. Ted Ohler and I teamed up for the past 10 years to run charters into the canyons out of Ocean City, Maryland.

Ted and I have bounced fishing strategies off each other while fishing, day after day. Our successful techniques proven by trial and error are incorporated into this book. Another highly successful team that has shared some of their successful secrets for this book is Captain Josh Ruskey and William (Willie) Zimmerman.

These two outstanding anglers teamed up to fish waters from the Mid Atlantic to Mexico. They know how to put fish in the boat. How good are they? They won just shy of a million dollars during 2005, in several tournaments. They are fishermen "in the know." I talked them into staying onshore one day and threw out some questions that may help anglers who want to catch billfish. Of course they agreed, after a little coercion—and my agreeing to pick up the tab up at the Tiki bar. Here's how our conversation went:

Unkart: What is the most important tip you could share for someone trying to catch a marlin?
Ruskey: Capitalize on each bite! I cannot emphasize this point enough.

Capt. Ted Ohler (far left) and author (far right) display's this happy angler's first white on his 18th birthday.

You are only going to have so many opportunities and cannot afford to waste any.

Zimmerman: I agree with Josh. There are days you may only have one shot and need to take advantage of and make the most of that bite.

Unkart. Can you give an example of capitalizing on a bite?

Zimmerman: Sure. You need to see the fish before the bite. Everyone needs to watch the spread. We divide the baits up, some people watch the port and others watch the starboard baits. By seeing the fish before it hits a bait in the spread, I increase our hook-up ratio to 90-percent.

Ruskey: Leave nothing to chance. Double and triple check each piece of equipment. We rig new wind ons before every tournament or any time a leader appears worn. Each bite could be worth big bucks or could be the catch of a lifetime, and no detail, regardless of how small, can be over-looked if you are going to capitalize on a bite.

Unkart: You change wind on leaders, what else do you do that leaves nothing to chance?

Ruskey: I do not use snap swivels. I use all crimps with welded ring ball bearing swivels. I don't know how, but snap swivels sometimes come open. By eliminating the snaps, it's one less thing that can go wrong. It is time consuming when changing rigs, but worth the effort. We check drag settings every day and any piece of terminal tackle in question is replaced.

Unkart: When you are constantly moving to different locations along the eastern seaboard how do you decide what areas to fish?

Ruskey: You do your homework. I keep a check on satellite views from Roffers for temperature breaks and pods of baitfish. I also count on local captains I know to share information on where the hot bite has been the past few days. Other then that, you fish areas that have produced for you in the past and fish methods that you know are productive.

Unkart: How many lines do you troll when using naturals?

Ruskey: Seven if I run a shotgun from the bridge.

Unkart: Only seven lines? I troll nine to 11.

Zimmerman: Yeah, but you really do not want to take a chance with that many lines. A lot of lines can cause confusion and foul up the works when a fish is in the spread. If you cannot get the attention of a fish with seven lines you are not going to do it with nine or more.

Unkart: Can you explain how to set the hook with naturals?

Zimmerman: Troll baits with the clicker on and just enough pressure to prevent a backlash. If you are not paying attention the reel lets you know there is a bite. When a fish comes on a natural, I jerk the bait away until he becomes aggressive. After he comes back on the bait and hits it, I free spool until he picks up the bait, then hit him hard. Then I slowly push the drag up to put pressure on him.

Ruskey: You want the clips set light when using naturals in case you do not see the fish. The bait needs to snap on his first hit.

Unkart: Anything you two can add to help fishermen catch a marlin?

Ruskey: Keep it fun and try to remain calm. Don't get upset.

Zimmerman: (looking at Josh) What? Don't get upset! (shaking his head in disbelief.) Josh is the guy who screams and yells every time something goes wrong. Hell, he changes shirts four times a day just for good luck. And if we are not raising fish he wants to know what I'm doing wrong. Now, he says don't get upset. I can't believe this!

I will not place into print the exchange that followed, after deciding it would be in the best interest of all concerned to terminate the interview before I ruined a successful fishing team.

Experienced anglers form methods of catching white marlin. What works for one angler does not necessarily mean it will works for the next. Then again, there are basics that everyone practices. Here are a few suggestions that I practice and feel are important to be successful.

• Artificials need to remain in the water to create a disturbance to attract marlin. An artificial flying out of the water and landing sideways is not going

A great fishing team, Capt. Willie Zimmerman (left) and Captain Josh Ruskey (right).

to raise fish. Many artificial lures are capable of being trolled at nine knots or more. However, this may not be their most productive speed. Watch how the lure runs in any given conditions, instead of setting the boat to your "normal" speed.

• Never give up on a favorite lure or bait that consistently produces. Even on slow days, pull the one or two lures or baits that normally produce fish. Pull these from sunup to sundown. As an example, when I am trolling the Mid Atlantic, there is always a Green Machine in the spread. It may be attached to a spreader bar or pulled alone as a lure. But, it is always behind the boat. It has produced that well for me over the years.

• Don't set lines then forget about them. Many times grass fouls the bait. The last thing an angler needs are baits that are not going to catch a fish. Rotate baits or lures every 30 to 45 minutes to find a bait location that produces. It is strange that a bait can be productive in the flat line position yet not raise fish on the short rigger, or vice versa. Only experimentation can pinpoint this type of information for you.

• KISS (Keep it simple stupid); do what you know works. There is nothing wrong with changing tactics and trying new things, but fish with the methods that you are knowledgeable about and feel most comfortable with.

SAILFISH

If blue marlin are the heavy weights of the billfish arena, sailfish are the lightweights. But, for what they lack in brute strength, they more then make up for as scrappy fighters at the end of the line. 30 class outfits are more then sufficient for subduing Istiophorus platypterus, with 20 pound line allowing anglers to experience everything a sailfish has to offer.

They can be found in the warm waters of the Gulf Stream from Massachusetts to the Keys. However, sails call the south coast of Florida home during the winter. The area from Palm Beach up to Fort Pierce is not called Sailfish Alley without good reason. Baitfish migrating south for the winter provide sails with an abundance of food, which in turn, provide anglers with up to 10 to 20 shots a day at fish. Stuart, Florida, which is in the middle of sailfish alley, lays claim to the title "Sailfish Capital of the World." This may be debatable, nonetheless, the pattern of winter bait available just offshore has been bringing sailfish to the area for years. Off Palm Beach, Stuart and Jupiter, sailfish are available year round, but there is superb fishing usually beginning in October and running through March. After March, many of the fish follow the warm Gulf Stream waters north to summer off Cape Hatteras, North Carolina, arriving sometime around May. Their numbers increase and peak during August or the beginning of September. Occasionally sailfish are caught further north, but their numbers do not justify targeting the species.

Sailfish are great for the light tackle enthusiast since spinning gear with 15- to 20-pound test line allows for spectacular aerial acrobatics. Capable of blistering runs at over 60-mph, they may be the fastest swimming short distance game fish, even beating wahoo to the finish line. Like the blue marlin, they are able to "light-up" when excited and display shimmering colors. They are easily identifiable from blue or white marlin by their exaggerated dorsal fin, which is approximately two times the height of the body. The dorsal fin also extends ¾ of the fish's length, making them one of the most beautiful billfish to pursue. Now, combine this beauty with the fact that unlike other billfish, they are not very picky eaters, hunt in packs, and can be caught in shallow water. You just may have the perfect billfish! Diets widely vary and include mackerel, small tuna, jacks, sardines, anchovies, herring, pilchards, blue runners, mullet, flying fish, and of course ballyhoo. All these baits are available off the Florida coast with the bait dejour being what is available at the time. Sailfish appear less pelagic then other billfish, probably due to baitfish migration being responsible for their

**Capt. Rob Skillman (left) of the charter boat *Endeavor*
and mate John Meade admire a nice sailfish before the release.**

presence more then their own migration patterns. When ballyhoo or other baitfish school up on inshore reefs, the sails follow, even into water only 30' deep. This is just the opposite of other billfish, which want deep water beneath them. When baitfish are scarce, the best bet is looking for them further offshore where they feed on flying fish, small tuna and other blue water baitfish.

Just a few short years ago, the method of catching sails was no different then that of other billfish. Teasers were used to raise fish with rigged ballyhoo or mullet being trolled. A pitch bait, ready for the bait and switch tactic with a teaser, was always ready. Trolling the edges of blue/green water, along with temperature breaks or weed lines, accounted for taking the most sails. The method worked then and still does today. However, in recent years live bait has taken over as the mainstay of catching sails. Part of this may be due to the increased use of circle hooks, being used to prevent damage to the fishery. In addition, live bait used with circle hooks creates a situation where even most novice charter clients can participate in hooking fish.

The nuts and bolts for fishing live bait is relatively simple. Begin by rigging in the following manner: Create a double line two feet long using a Spider Hitch or Bimini Twist. Attach approximately 12' of 60- to 80-pound leader material using an Albright knot; most sailfishermen will use fluorocarbon. To the leader attach a suitable circle hook for the bait size. This normally will be a 6/0 or 7/0 hook.

Rig conventional outfits in the same manner or use one of the new small barrel swivels in place of the double line. A small egg weight of one ounce or so may be used to add weight to help keep the line in the water. A float can be placed on the line to suspend the bait near the surface, or tie a ribbon to the line 15' from the swivel. This allows you to see how deep the bait is when being fished off a kite.

Fishing with live bait certainly gets the heart pumping when the bait comes to the surface and nervously tries to escape the predator below. When the bait surfaces, get prepared!

Remember when using circle hooks to point the rod at the fish and count to three after the sail takes the bait. Wind until the line comes tight and the fish reacts by stripping line. Then raise the rod tip and begin your fight. If the line does not come tight, immediately stop winding—many times the fish will come back on the bait, or when small packs are working bait, another sail will gobble it down.

Kites have become extremely popular when sailfishing. Set the spread by using two baits off a kite. Many knowledgeable anglers use two kites, fishing two lines from each. It does take work attending to a kite.

When the wind does not cooperate, trolling slowly into a slight breeze is also effective.

You don't have a kite, or you just do not want the hassle of fishing with them? Not a problem. Use a float and suspend the bait beneath. The float does not seem to affect the sails and a disappearing float certainly tells anglers that the fish has the bait.

Sailfish have no problem feeding on the surface, but occasionally become finicky and prefer deep baits. For this reason, always suspend a bait at 50', or half way to the bottom if in shallower water. This bait is now doing double-duty and is in a prime area for wahoo or kings. Due to this fact, and if you want to tangle with one of these toothy critters the deep line should be rigged with a 12" section of wire leader to prevent bite offs.
When a stiff breeze is blowing out of the north and sailfish are tailing or riding the waves, slow-troll live bait off the outriggers and run two flat lines. As you move north up to Hatteras, most fishermen switch over from live bait to trolling rigged naturals. The key for success is to slow down when trolling. Sails do not find baits trolled at six or more knots very appetizing. Three or four knots produces more action. Look for current edges where blue and green water clash, which attracts baitfish and the sails. Once a sailfish is hooked up, work the area hard. It is seldom that there will be only one since they seem to migrate in small groups or packs. And when you hook up a sail, do not clear the other lines immediately. Leave them in the water for a few minutes. This accounts for multiple hook-ups.

Captain Ted Ohler likes to fish out of Fort Pierce for sails. He offers the following six tips for success:

1. Use live bait.
2. Slow troll. It outproduces drift fishing and covers more area.
3. Only troll fast enough to keep the bait from tangling. The bait must be allowed to swim, not be pulled through the water.
4. Live mullet are the number one choice bait, with ballyhoo close behind.
5. Keep rigging simple. Use a circle hook and rig live bait by hooking only in the top lip. This allows the bait to inhale water and pass it over the gills, so it lives longer on the hook.
6. Use a large spread, and do not pull flat lines close to the boat.

SHARK

I can remember when catching 20 or more sharks a day was typical. Unfortunately, sharks have come under a lot of fishing pressure over

Fishermen always get excited when catching a nasty mouth of teeth!

the past few decades from the commercial end, as well as recreational fishermen. Catches in the numbers of "the good old days" seldom occurs currently. Nonetheless, it is still a good fishery that makes for a very fun and unpredictable day offshore. Currently, fishermen are prohibited from possessing very many species of sharks. Only one shark per vessel with a minimum size of 54" and one Atlantic sharpnose shark per person is allowed to be harvested at this time. Make sure to check federal possession regulations before venturing offshore, as regulations change often.

A shark's growth rate is slow. Many species take 12 to 18 years to mature. Long reproductive cycles, anywhere from one to two years, result in small numbers of young. This all contributes to the difficult time the fishery has trying to recuperate from over-fishing. The senseless killing of sharks by recreational fishermen who want a set of jaws should be avoided. Practice catch and release, keeping a shark only when wanted for consumption. However, if the shark is not cared for properly when caught, anglers will be disappointed in the flavor of the meat.

Sharks are without a urinary tract, causing urea to concentrate in the blood before being excreted through the skin. Urea is a by-product of protein metabolism. Unfortunately, it is converted by bacteria to ammonia once the shark dies. Improper handling of a shark causes a strong ammonia odor and taste. Sharks must be dressed and bled right after catching to prevent the urea from breaking down into the meat. It does not take a lot of intelligence to figure out that a mouth full of angry teeth and an angler armed with a knife is not a good mix! Safety must be the first priority when handling a shark being kept for consumption. If you are serious about catching sharks for consumption, invest in a bang stick to subdue them, instead of a gun. Carrying a firearm onboard can be a danger in itself. A boat rocking with a loaded gun in hand can have negative consequences. At the very least, do not attempt to dress-out the shark until it at least appears to be dead. Then remember, a shark's nervous system is capable of causing an involuntary jaw snapping reaction, even a couple hours after appearing dead. Use caution even with "dead" sharks!

The number one targeted species of shark by recreational fishermen is mako. This chapter's information applies to that species. However, the recommendations for catching mako apply to just about any type of shark that happens to find your bait.

Unlike other types of sharks, mako (Isurus oxyrhincus) are considered a gamefish. I use the word gamefish since they are capable of spectacular jumps and smoking reels. Not able to swim the speed of bill-

Emily is all smiles after catching her first mako.

fish, they still can obtain speeds in the mid-20s and use all this speed after being hooked. This often ends in the mako skyrocketing two or three times their length out of the water. Pound for pound, they are not able to complete with the pulling duration that a tuna exerts, but nonetheless, mako certainly can test an angler's skill. Although mako over 1,000 pounds are occasionally caught, the norm is 100 to 300 pounds. 50 class outfits are more then adequate for the average mako. Serious shark fishermen, in pursuit of large tackle-busting sharks, often up equipment size to 80 or 130 pound tackle. This certainly is recommended if targeting extremely large predators.

Mako tolerate water in the upper 50s, but for best results try to locate water from 62 to 65 degrees. In the Mid Atlantic, as warming ocean temperatures reach into the 60s—which corresponds with the migration of bluefish—anglers know mako should be feeding and in the vicinity.

When rigging for sharks, it goes without saying that the teeth are the number one cause for concern. The tip of a shark's tooth can exert over 40,000 pounds of pressure per square inch. Just using wire leader is not sufficient. Stranded wire leader may work for smaller sharks, but larger sets of teeth are able to bite through each strand one at a time until you are left with a frown on the face. Use solid wire leader. Although single-strand wire has a tendency to kink in lighter gauges, I have never encountered a problem when using number 12, 180 pound test Malin hard-wire. Number 15 may

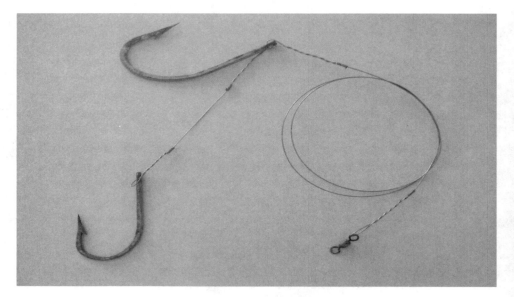

A common two hook shark rig

also be used (278 pound test,) but it is more difficult to work with. Use wire for the first three feet of leader to which the hook(s) are attached. Then install a barrel swivel on the other end, for connecting to the remaining leader.

Hook size should be consistent with bait and targeted shark size. A shark mouth full of teeth gets lot of attention. Many anglers assume sharks have large mouths and large hooks are required. In fact, this is not the case. Do not get me wrong, a 600-pound mako has no problem inhaling a good size bait and hook, but when you are dealing with 150-pounders, which is more often then not what is caught, the hook and bait needs to be on the smaller side. I prefer a two hook set-up. For large sharks, the main hook is a 14/0 with an 11/0 trailer. Smaller shark rigs get an 11/0 with a 9/0 trailer.

This hook and leader set-up is then attached in one of two ways to leader material. I like using 12' of 400-pound mono. This is crimped to the barrel swivel of the hook leader, with another barrel swivel attached to the other end for connection to the fishing line. Mono is easy to work with and flexible when a shark becomes entangled and twists the leader around its body. This gives you 15' of leader, which is more then adequate to prevent the tail of even a thresher shark from getting through the line when swimming directly away from you. The other alternative rigging method is to use 12' of 7-strand or preferably 49-strand wire. Even when targeting smaller sharks, by staying with a 15' leader, larger sharks can be fought without fear of line separation caused by the tail.

Weight is required to suspend dead bait beneath a float. It is extremely important to attach the weight to the leader beneath the line swivel. This keeps the line swivel straight. If the weight is attached to the fishing line itself, the line and leader twist and tangle around the swivel. Electrical tape may be used to secure the lead weight to the line. In this manner, the weight pulls off on the bite. Large foam floats may be used to suspend baits and are used by many shark fishermen. Personally, I do not care for the drag they create while battling a shark. Balloons are used as floats, but some anglers don't like using them because they may be detrimental to the environment. What is the alternative? Purchase a couple six-foot pool noodles which are made of foam, for a buck a piece. Cut them into six-inch pieces and attach one to the line by use of a rubber band. Once the bite occurs, the float comes free during the first run.

Sharks have an uncanny sense of smell, capable of detecting odors at great distances. To put it in simple terms, sharks can smell about 10,000 times better then a human! Due to this fact, by placing an appetizing scent in the water, anglers can increase their chances of success. The main two types of chum are menhaden and mackerel. Both emit oil which causes a slick, which on calm days can be seen and smelled by a shark for miles.

Chum normally can be purchased frozen in five-gallon buckets. Cut two or three holes in the bucket and suspend it over the side of the boat. The rocking of the boat keeps the chum coming out and attracting sharks. A five-gallon bucket in 65-degree water lasts about three to four hours.

Early in the season, set up for Mako in locations where their food is concentrated. The 20 fathom line normally holds bluefish migrating north and is an ideal location to set up. Even out to the 30 fathom line is productive. Further south, target cooler water or fish the deep.

Fish four lines with bait suspended at 15', 30', 45', and one line just below the thermocline. A rod should also be ready in case the mako passes up the baits and comes to the chum bucket. This is where a pitch bait comes in handy and is often picked up by the curious mako. As mentioned before, when deciding on bait, keep in mind the size of sharks in the area. It is difficult to beat fresh bait. A fresh filet of bluefish is an enticing bait, as are mackerel. When fresh is not available, frozen mackerel certainly works. Live bait is also ideal for shark fishing. Use a kite to suspend a live bait splashing around on the surface. A live bluefish makes a great bait when targeting big mako. Remember to give the shark time to swallow large baits like bluefish. It will take two or three bites, so do not be in a hurry to set the hook. Spot, menhaden or any of the other baitfish fished live also works for shark.

Setting the hook is accomplished by using a few sharp hard sets. The mouth on a shark is unlike other gamefish. It is hard and fear of pulling the hook through the mouth area is not of concern.

Landing a shark can be more of a battle then the fight itself at times. A flying gaff simplifies the procedure. A tail rope is essential to secure the shark to the boat. Tail ropes need to have a 10' piece of cable wire which is then attached to the rope itself. Sharks have no problem biting through ½" or ¼" line when used as a tail rope.

Finally, do not bring a live shark aboard the boat for the obvious reasons, which I explained in the opening chapter—it's just plain dangerous. Instead, if your boat is equipped with a swim platform, they make an ideal location to secure a shark for the ride home. If your boat has a sturdy tower you can use a block and tackle to lift the shark out of the water, and strap it to the tower structure. Shark can also be hung on the outside of the transom by suing a tail rope on one end and a flying gaff on the other. Tie off the shark at water level, and once the boat is up on plane, the shark will ride suspended in the air.

SKIPJACK

Katsuwonus pelamis are not pursued by many fishermen along the Atlantic coastline where they are plentiful, and usually they are an incidental catch. Referred to as striped tuna, arctic bonito, oceanic bonito or more commonly called skippies, recreational fishermen often pass the opportunity to catch the species due to size. Being one of the smaller tuna they cannot measure up against other relatives of the family. In the Pacific, however, they are commercially harvested and sold frozen or canned.

Skipjack are identifiable by the four to six prominent longitudinal stripes on the belly back towards the tail. Found throughout the Atlantic seaboard from Maine to Florida, they tend to migrate farther offshore then the false albacore or bonito. Schools of these small tuna, often seen breaking surface early in the day by anglers en route to offshore fishing grounds, are passed by. Those seen in the deep, where hopes arise of larger fish feeding upon them for dinner, may attract more interest. Marlin, mako and large tuna include skippies in their diet. Fishermen are a different story. Due to their relatively small size and the unappealing look of their bloody red flesh, most fishermen do not seek them out. However, skipjack meat is mild compared to the red meat of false albacore. It can be eaten raw, baked, broiled and also used in tuna salad.

Darren Selznich, on the right, owner of Ole Florida Fly shop in Boca Raton, Fl, and David Phillips proudly display a double header of skippies taken while fishing with Captain Scott Hamilton. Photo courtesy of Fly Fishing Extremes.

The fish may be targeted with small lures representing baitfish or whatever is being fed upon. When one is hooked and caught, a quick check of what is in the stomach contents informs anglers of what type of bait to imitate when casting artificial lures. When breaking water, the fish normally feeds against the current. Position the boat up-current and cast down to the school. Keep offerings on the small side—it is a waste of time casting or trolling baits intended for larger species.

After catching enough for consumption, save a few for dolphin bait. Skippies cut up into small pieces work well for bailing dolphin. Also, if targeting blue marlin or mako shark, this small member of the tuna family makes an excellent live bait under a kite. They may also be rigged for trolling and are a first class pitch-bait for blue marlin.

SWORDFISH

It becomes an obsession to chase and battle the ocean's gladiator. The swordfish bill is the largest of all the bills on fish. This broad weapon,

**Swordfish like this are why anglers
venture offshore into the darkness.**

used to stun or kill food, is prized by many fishermen and found proudly displayed in many trophy rooms. Xiphias gladius can be found throughout the deep waters of the continental shelf under the darkness of night. Dedicated fishermen constantly try to come up with better ways to catch this brute of the sea. However, before casting off lines and expecting to come back with swordfish steaks for the grill, there first needs to be some preparation.

The fishery is very similar to that of sharks, in that it is on the rebound. However, swords may have a better chance due their reproduction ability. According to the NMFS, by placing a 47" minimum size limit in 1999 and closing some areas to longline fishing, which included the nursery area off Florida's coastline in 2001, the population of swords has increased. Unfortunately, females do not reach maturity until around age four or five, at which time they weigh approximately 150 to 200 pounds. The average fish caught by recreational fishermen is well below this size. In 1960 the average size of swordfish caught was 266 pounds, yet in 1996 it was 90 pounds. With an average life span of around nine years, large females are needed to keep the stock healthy. On a positive note, females are capable of producing up to 30,000,000 eggs each year. Given the chance, swordfish should make a strong comeback.

Fishing for swordfish requires a HMS Angling permit, as does other billfish, shark, and tuna. One sword per angler is currently allowed with a 47" minimum, and a maximum of three per boat. Fishermen should practice catch and release, taking only that which is going to be consumed, as this in itself will help assure a bright future the fishery.

Although swordfish are sometimes seen basking on the surface and occasionally are caught during daylight, they spend most of their time in deep water. One look at the large pupil of the eye explains why they are caught at night. They are extremely sensitive to light. Their retinas are equipped with rods which allow sight in low-light conditions, making the fish capable of seeing light at great distances. Swords are able to withstand large temperature and depth swings. They are known to swim as deep as 2100'. Their optimum temperature range seems to be around 55- to 65-degrees, but during feeding, food dictates what temperature the fish will be found in. Their feeding at night in the vertical water column is also affected by available moonlight. Rule of thumb; the brighter the night, the deeper the bait. This is not due to the eyesight of the sword, but has more to do with baitfish itself. The brighter the night, the deeper baitfish tend to stay, which in turn dictates where predators feed. Locating the depth of baitfish on the fish finder is the first step when deciding what depth to target bait. Concentrate a couple lines at this depth. However, it is always prudent to set out a spread covering the vertical water column until fish are located.

Swords are seldom found in shallow waters, so begin your offshore search in 300 fathoms or more.

As with most types of fishing, Florida fishermen tend to lean towards live bait such as blue runners, goggle eyes and probably the best bait, tinker mackerel. Moving north, fishermen slowly switch over to dead bait, which includes mackerel, bonito and the number one bait, squid. While southern fishermen score well with live bait, the Mid Atlantic and northeast regions seem to score with rigged dead bait. Always have a small rod or two available when sword fishing to catch live bait. The light under or around the boat attracts squid and baitfish.

Rigging up for swordfish can be an art in itself. Ask several sword fishermen how to rig and each will give you a different method with the exception of two rules: First, a light source needs to be used near the bait to attract swords; and second, the float and weight on your rigs need to break away after the hook-up.

Outside of these two necessities, experiment with rigging until you find what works for you. Like the variety of methods used to troll for billfish or tuna, there are different methods that all work for swords. I like using wind-on leaders whenever possible in all my fishing. This takes wiring a fish out of equation during landing, makes for a safer environment for fishermen in daylight, and certainly reduces chances for injury while fishing in the darkness for swords.

Swords are brutes on the end of the line. Tackle for swords requires at least 50 class outfits. Begin the rigging process by marking the lines. Darkness makes every task more difficult, but by tying a two-inch piece of wax line at 50', 100', 200', and 300', the setting of lines is not such a chore. Wax line secures very well to monofilament with very little slippage when running in and out of the rod guides. Once lines are marked, decide in what fashion to attach the wind-on. The rigging section of the book explains methods, and in this case can be by using a 150-pound barrel swivel that's able to pass through the rods guides, or by tying a Bimini or Spider Hitch to create a double line for attaching a wind-on leader loop to loop. Another choice is to use an Albright knot to secure the fishing line to the leader. Leader poundage should be 250 to 300, and it should be around 10' in length. At the end of the leader, crimp a 300-pound ball bearing swivel. Then crimp another six-foot piece of leader material and a hook. Crimp the hook to the leader. Hook size can vary depending on bait size, but should be in the 9/0 to 13/0 range. Use a strong, hardened hook, because swordfish are powerful and have no problem straightening cheaper quality steel hooks.

Another point for consideration is how the point of the hook is sharpened. The swordfish mouth is nothing like their cousins; they have soft mouths. Do not sharpen the hook into a cutting point, instead shape a round point coming to needle-sharpness for penetration. A cutting edge sharpened onto the hook creates a hole in the soft mouth tissue during the hook-set, which may later allow the fish to throw the hook.

Once the bait is affixed to the hook, the next step is to attach the light source. Use a chemical light stick (cylume) and attach it with a number 64 rubber band 10' above the hook. Many anglers only use one stick per bait. Try using three per bait. Attach the first at 10' from the bait then spaced the others two feet apart. The additional lights seems to help attract fish. Green is by far the favorite color, but blue is being used more and more with success.

Slowly let the line out until coming to the first piece of wax line. This you know is at 50', so attach your weight by using a number 64 rubber band. The rubber band is able to hold a pound of weight without slipping, assuming you pull it snugly to the line. The amount of weight to use depends on sea conditions, currents etc. Seldom will you be able to get away with less then a pound; two pounds is common. 90-percent of the time the weight snaps off after the bite, allowing the fish to be fought without concern. Now, continue letting line out until you reach the fourth piece of wax line. At this point you know you have 300' of line out. This is where you attach a float. If using a balloon, you can place a chemical light inside it to increase visibility in the darkness. Blow it up and attach it to the line. The balloon may be tied directly to the line by using a snug half-hitch, or a #64 rubberband may be used to secure it. The piece of wax line previously installed on the line assists by not allowing the balloon to slip. By using different color chemical sticks in the balloons, you can keep track of the lines in the darkness. Instead of balloons, milk jugs may also be used. Chemical sticks can again be installed inside the jug, which is secured to the line with a rubber band. Another option, the one I prefer, is to use the pool noodles. Use a two-foot piece which is attached to the line with a rubber band. Now, place a chemical stick inside an empty 16-ounce water bottle and press the bottle into the hole in the noodle—you'll have a float where the light is a foot above the water, making the line easy to watch.

After attaching the float, let the rig drift a couple hundred feet from the boat and then continue the setup procedure with the next three lines. Use staggered depths and distances from the boat for each line. The task is easy since the lines are marked. The forth and last line does not need a float, just place it 50' below the boat. A light source, such as a Hydro-Glow fluorescent light placed under the boat, works well to attract swords to this bait. The Hydro-Glow combined with the chemical stick on the shallow line accounts for a good percentage of the bites.

Now that the lines are set, a decision must be made on how the drags are set. The point is a matter of personnel preference. The two schools of thought are to set the drag light with only enough tension to prevent a backlash, or set the reel at strike position. Setting the drag light is thought to prevent the sword from dropping the bait since resistance from the drag is minimal. I discount the theory, feeling the fish still feels the resistance from a pound of lead when the bait is picked up. I prefer the reel to be set in strike position. When the fish picks up the bait and runs, the drag sets the hook, the same as when fishing for kings. This technique works especially well if circle hooks are used. If the float's light is observed moving, pick the rod up and wait until pressure is felt, and at that point begin winding to set the hook.

Swordfish often pick a bait up slowly and hold it before swallowing. Do not be in a hurry, but wait for the fish to swim off. It is not recommended to set the hook. The soft mouth of a sword does not hold up well to a lot of pressure, which brings up to another point: what poundage to set the drags. Many anglers believe the 25- to 30-percent setting is too much pressure for swordfish, and if the hook does not secure in a hard part of the mouth or into the base of the bill, too much drag accounts for pulled hooks. I for one believe that if I am going to pull a hook I want to do it in the beginning of a fight, and not two hours later. There is good argument for both sides. By setting the drag at eight pounds you'll fight the fish longer, and may not pull the hook. With a heavier drag the hook may pull, but if it doesn't in the beginning of the battle, chances are it is secure enough to land the fish in less time.

Stomachs checked on swords indicate that they slash and stun their prey before eating, since the fish that are swallowed appear to have gone down head first. For this reason, when you see a float bobbing around or moving, have patience and wait until pressure is felt to begin winding. Allow the time for the bait to be eaten completely.

On the first run after the hook up, the sinker and float normally break away when secured to the line with rubber bands. If not, they are easily cut off when they come to the rod tip. Any light sticks remaining on the line as the fish is brought to the boat can be slide down to the crimped swivel as the angler continues to wind the swivel to the rod tip, until the gaff can be sunk. This is a crucial and dangerous time of the catch. The bill is a weapon protruding from the front of a sword. It is capable of piecing a body and causing serious injury. Stories of bills penetrating bodies and boat hulls make one wonder if fish have emotion and know about revenge. While we believe this not to be true, extreme caution must be used. Be conscience of

This Golden tilefish caught by Capt. Ron Callis on the charter boat Reel Addiction would have set a new world record tipping the scale at 60 pounds! But, Ron was using an electric reel—which disqualifies the fish.

the bill and always hold it to the outside to your body, never in front of your torso. One powerful flick of the tail and the results could be injurious.

Finally, your best chances for success come while fishing a few days after a full moon. The second best time period is three or four days before the full moon. Sword fishing is not for everyone. This is a sport that contains 95-percent boredom, sitting around waiting. But oh what a great five percent of pandemonium, when someone yells "fish on!"

TILEFISH

Fishing for tilefish is not rocket science. It is like bottom fishing for sea bass or any other inshore species, with the exception that you have a long wind. Maybe not one of the most popular fish in the ocean nor the most sought after, tilefish are a table delight and are quickly gaining popularity. Until you get hooked (pardon the pun) on fishing for tiles, it seems a waste to run 50 or more miles offshore just to bottom fish. Especially when you must wind up over 500' of line each time you want to check your bait. Nonetheless, offshore fishermen are warming up to tilefish.

Tilefish seem to prefer a soft or muddy bottom. However, until specific locations are identified, it is difficult to know or tell the bottom texture when searching for fish in 100 fathoms of water. Purests use electric reels, which any angler, after winding up his or her line five or six times, will agree may be worth the expense. Two pounds of lead on the end of your line can get heavy, even without a fish. Search out tilefish in 550' to 650' of water. Once an area has been identified as being productive, it will normally give fish up the majority of the time.

The rig is fairly simple and not difficult to construct. Use 100- to 250-pound mono and crimp four or five three-way swivels about a foot apart. To these attach 10/0 circle hooks on six-inch leaders. One end of the rig receives a barrel swivel, the other a heavy snap swivel. I recommend crimping everything.

Two pounds of weight is normally sufficient to reach bottom, but there are times with strong currents that something more substantial may be required, like a sash weight.

Squid are without a doubt the best bait, followed by fresh cut fish or clams. Butterfish are also decent bait. The new braided lines with their thin diameters are ideal for reaching down into the depths necessary to catch tilefish. They also provide a better feel than monofilament. Once the bite is felt, remember that with circle hooks, all you do is wind. Many anglers who specialize in tilefish also like to use a chemical light stick attached to the top of their rig to attract fish, just as when sword fishing.

If you find yourself offshore and the pelagic species normally pursued have lockjaw, try bouncing bottom a couple times and see if you can catch the tilefish fever.

TUNA – ALBACORE (LONGFIN)

Thunnus alalunga may not be the largest member of the tuna family, but they more then make up for their lack of size with an appetite that often fills the kill box. Commonly know as "white meat" tuna, as table fare they are excellent. The meat, being less oily then other tuna, is often packaged canned.

It is surprising that more anglers do not pursue longfin tuna. This may be partially due to the tuna favoring cooler waters and its availability increasing once other species of tuna have left in search of warmer waters.

Longfin will tolerate and feed in water at cool as 60-degrees, with 62 to 65 being the optimum temperature.

One look at the tuna and it is plain to see why they are called longfin. The pectoral fins are two times the length of those found on other members of the tuna family. Although not as large as their cousins, do not sell longfin short.

Tackle requirements do not have to be stout with fish size seldom tipping the scale past 40 pounds. 30 class outfits are more then capable of handing the chore of taming longfin. However, they will test even the most avid anglers. Longfin can be caught by trolling or by chunking and they are also susceptible to jigging. Seldom found on the inshore shoals, begin your search for feeding schools from the 50 fathom line on out into the deep waters of the canyons. It is always wise to begin looking for the fish by trolling. Once located, the school can be worked by trolling or by switching over to chunking.

Sorry, Charlie... you're headed for the grill.

Trolling for longfin is no different than trolling for yellowfin or bluefin, except that the pattern may be tightened up behind the boat. Captain Rob Skillman, who runs the *Endeavor*, makes catching longfin easy with this one tip: "Just remember the word green when it comes to catching longfin tuna." Green Machines, green spreader bars and green Tuna Clones normally are all that's required to put fish in the boat. Of course, ballyhoo or other rigged natural bait work as well, with squid being the number one rigged bait choice.

Longfin tuna do not appear to stay in the top layer of water above the thermocline as often as yellowfin and bluefin. More tolerable of cooler water, they are often found below it. If the fish are seen on the fish finder but are reluctant to come to the surface to feed, then chunking for them may be a good choice.

Offshore action can be fast and furious as late-season tuna fatten up for their migration. If fishing the Mid Atlantic northward in the late season, one thing will obviously be missing—other boats. The lack of radio chatter, normal during the summer, leaves you feeling on some days that you are the only boat in the ocean. If you observe three or four boats working an area do not hesitate to move in. Fishing offshore in the late season is like a brotherhood; if you are there you belong. Apparently the cold weather warms the hearts of charter captains. Try contacting them on the radio, and most will be more than happy to share some information this time of the year. Once you arrive at your intended fishing location, if there are no blips on the radar indicating other boats, there is no choice except start watching the fish finder to locate fish. It is not unusual to observe fish at 100' to 300' down, but the magic number seems to be around 200'. When the fish are observed on the finder, waste no time in throwing chunks of bait into the water and concentrate two or more lines at the depth where the fish were observed. In the worst-case scenario, if tuna cannot be found, pick an edge somewhere along the 100 fathom line and drift with lines staggered at different depths or go back to trolling until fish are located.

In order to suspend baits at 200' or more with a current and or breeze, heavy weight may be necessary. Rig lines with multiple eight-ounce egg sinkers; two to four may be necessary depending on the conditions. Secure sinkers from sliding on the line with a rubber band at least 50' from the bait. A six-foot piece of 50 pound fluorocarbon with a 9/0 circle hook attached to a quality swivel rounds out the rig. Remember, slowly lower the rig to prevent tangling. If the spool is disengaged and the line allowed to come off the reel too quickly, the bait will wrap around the line. You need to control the decent, to prevent this occurrence.

Chunk by throwing a few pieces over at a time, and once they are

This bigeye was caught at night on a live squid, fished in Baltimore Canyon.

out of sight, throw another handful. When a longfin is hooked deep and brought up, often the school follows it to the surface. It is now imperative to continue chunking while fish are being caught. Once a school is behind the boat, it can provide all the action a group of anglers can handle.

Another option is to use diamond jigs. When longfin are observed on the depth finder, drop the jigs to that depth and work with short quick jerks. No hits? Wind up 10' and begin jerking again. If longfin are observed feeding on the surface, artificial lures such as feather jigs can be very effective when cast and retrieved quickly.

TUNA – BIGEYE

Maybe we should refer to this fish as Mr. Bigeye instead of Thunnus obesus, since they are often more than most anglers can handle. Tackle-busting ability and the determination of a mad dog when on the end of the fishing line has earned this member of the tuna family a title of respect.

If you believe bluefin tuna and yellowfin tuna are difficult to tell apart, then it is very likely bigeye tuna will have you scratching your head as well.

With a body shaped like a bluefin and pectoral fins the length of a yellowfin, identification can be difficult. There are a few ways that an angler can tell the difference. First and foremost are the eyes. The pupil of a bigeye is almost two times the diameter of the other two species, thus its name. Of course, if there is not another tuna to compare the eyes and you have had little experience with bigeye, then you must move on to another indicator. Next examine the fins. The pectoral fins on a bigeye are almost identical in length to that of the yellowfin, extending to the beginning of the second dorsal fin.

Since this really does not distinguish the bigeye from large yellow-fin, take a look at the anal fin. This fin is shorter on bigeye then on mature yellowfin, which tend to be long. Still unsure? Examine the body. More often than not, the body will contain lateral iridescent blue bands on the side, which bluefin and yellowfin lack. However, this characteristic must be checked as soon as the fish comes out of the water, since the lines fade after death. If there is still a question as to the identity of the tuna lying on the floor of the cockpit, location caught may be the final identifying feature. Bigeye are seldom caught inside the 100 fathom line. This member of the tuna family likes a lot of water beneath it as it searches out dinner in or near the Gulf Stream, along the Continental Shelf. Recreational fishermen often do not target bigeye since they tend to inhabit the deep ocean canyons far offshore. Also, the quality of their meat is also in question. The flesh or meat of bigeye contains a high concentration of fat, giving it a different flavor then bluefin or yellowfin. Nonetheless, the excitement surrounding catching a bigeye more then overshadows long offshore runs or the lack of excellent table fare.

There is usually no mistaking a bigeye bite. Averaging 100 to 200 pounds, these fish leave a huge hole in the ocean on the bite. Unlike other members of the tuna family who often come up underneath the bait and snatch it, a bigeye bite usually results in a huge explosion on the bait. These fish hit in multiples very often, resulting in two or three anglers having their hands full. This results in total chaos in the pit, which after all is one of the reasons we fish!

Bigeye tuna are susceptible to discomfort from bright sunlight. This results in many bites developing early in the morning or evening. When bigeye are frequenting an area, it may be necessary to draw them to the surface. One of the best methods for doing this is to use spreader bars. They seem to be attracted to disturbances of the water, especially near the transom of the boat. Due to this fact, when targeting big eyes, run a tight spread. Spreader bars off of the short riggers along with one pulled as a center flat line may be just the trick for raising these tuna.

A great blackfin taken off the Florida coast.

Of course, they are susceptible to rig baits as well. Remember, the average bigeye tipping the scale at 100 or more pounds does not mind attacking big bait. Ballyhoo, mullet, and squid positioned around the spreader bars increase hookup percentages.

TUNA – BLACKFIN

Thunnus atlanticus is one the smallest members of the tuna family and is probably the most easy to distinguish. The top of the fish near the dorsal fin is bluish-black in color. Unlike other members of the tuna family, the most reliable identifying characteristic is the color of the small finlets located behind the dorsal and anal fins. The other four species of tuna find these fins yellow, however on the blackfin, they are distinctively dusky in color with only a tinge of a yellowish tint. Most prominent from Florida northward to the Outer Banks, this school fish does not have a large following. This is probably due to its lack of size. Averaging five to 10 pounds does not place a demand on the fish by recreational fishermen nor place them at the top of the popularity list, although they are good to eat and a decent scrapper on light tackle. Being a school fish, they are ideal for catching on light tackle with live bait. However, most encounters with blackfin come as incidental catches while fishing for one of their cousins.

**This bluefin tipped the scale at 225
pounds and fell for a whole butterfish
set five cranks off the bottom.**

If they show up in good numbers on your stomping grounds, keep bait on the smaller side. Use four- to five-inch Tuna Clone type lures or feathers for trolling. The mini Green Machine is also productive. Blackfin also find just about any type of live bait appetizing, even shrimp.

TUNA - BLUEFIN

Thunnus thynnus, the big dog, and not only because it is the biggest member of the tuna family. You have heard the saying, "if you can't run with the big dogs stay on the porch!" Well that certainly applies to the bluefin. Pound for pound, there is no other member of the tuna family that is going to put a hurtin' on an angler like bluefin tuna. If your idea of a fantastic fishing day is feeling like somebody has beat the hell out of you, then bluefin is your fish. Their no-quit attitude at the end of the line has probably accounted for more sore muscles then any other fish. Bluefin are near the top of my list when it comes to favorite fish to catch. This is probably due to the success ratio I've had when pursuing bluefin. While other charter boats chase yellowfin tuna, I like to stick with bluefin and have done so with great success. Federal regulations prevent us from keeping as many bluefin as yellowfins, but their size more than make up for the lack of numbers.

My brother-in-law, Charlie Cook, was pretty smug one day as I pulled up to the scales. His charter had already docked and weighed their nine yellowfin tuna and was doing a little celebrating. The good-natured kidding immediately started since I was only flying three tuna flags. Charlie was quick to bring to my attention they had tipped the scales with 350-pounds of yellowfin. But the last laugh was to be mine when the dock master called out the weight of our three fish, which was 419-pounds! That's a perfect example of why I like to fish for bluefin instead of yellowfin, and why repeat customers always ask if bluefin are around.

Bluefin tuna are extremely unique, unlike other members of the tuna family. They are very adept at adjusting body temperature to the surrounding water. Being able to do this allows them to feed throughout the water column, especially near the bottom on inshore shoals. As I mentioned earlier with yellowfin, it is beneficial to understand the quarry you pursue. This is very true with the bluefin tuna. The Tuna Research and Conservation Center, in cooperation with several universities, did an extensive survey on tracking bluefin tuna with satellite technology. Their findings, although not targeted at the recreational angler, nonetheless can make us better bluefin fishermen.

In this study, bluefin tuna caught off North Carolina were tagged with pop-off satellite tags, before they were released. The tag stayed on the fish anywhere from 60 to 90 days, after which it detached from the fish and floated to the surface. The information stored in the tags was then transmitted to the ARGO satellite system. The information is not only interesting, but gives us a better understanding of how tuna behave within their environment. Bluefin tuna travel remarkable distances. The farthest distance covered in 90 days was 1670 nautical miles. One tuna traveled 1242 nautical miles in 60 days. This data tells us that some bluefin traveled an average of over 20 miles each day!

Temperature preference data indicates that tuna have extraordinary tolerances for temperature swings. Bluefin were found to spend time in temperatures ranging from 42.8- to 75.2-degrees. One of the tuna's daily average was 51.8-degrees for 60 days. Even with staying in this cooler water, bluefin are able to maintain a body temperature of 77- to 80-degrees. This ability to conserve metabolic heat allows bluefin to be caught in waters that we, as anglers, would normally not place our baits. Specifically, below the thermocline and near the bottom. Available food is probably a better indicator of where bluefin can be found, compared to water temperatures.

Another satellite tagging study showed that bluefin spend 40 percent of their time in the top 30' layer of water during summer when water temperatures are the warmest. During the winter, when there are mixed layers of water, the vertical distribution of tuna expanded towards deeper water. I find this extremely interesting and draw the conclusion that bluefin tuna do not spend the majority of their time above the thermocline at anytime of the year. In addition, the fish showed distinctive vertical movement during periods of dawn and dusk. After dawn, tuna make a very slow and steady descent to a depth of approximately 82' from near the surface. Remarkably, it took the bluefin approximately 40 minutes to achieve this depth movement. Just the opposite was observed at dusk, where the fish took approximately 40 minutes to rise near the surface. This information should give anglers an idea of where to place baits.

Studies such as these provide an eye-opening amount of knowledge. I look forward to the day when this type of information can be available for all the species we pursue. One reason so much time, effort and money is placed into bluefin studies is due to their commercial value and declining numbers. Researchers are trying to gain information in order to secure the fishery. Now let us take this information and put it to use for our benefit.

As with yellowfin, trolling is the number one way recreational anglers attempt catch bluefin. Your trolling pattering needs to vary depending on the size of bluefin available that time of the season. Small bluefin find cedar plugs, Zukers and rig baits pulled right off the transom appetizing. Larger bluefin, on the other hand, are not as apt to take flat lines. Short and long riggers will produce most of the fish. Also, a way, way back line is very productive. Large bluefin find a large naked ballyhoo or triple Green Machine daisy chain placed in this position difficult to pass up. This is not to say that larger bluefin will not attack flat lines. On any given day it is impossible to say how fish are going to feed behind the boat. But until this knowledge is learned for that day, it is a wise choice to start with what normally works.

Spreader bars are very effective for bluefin with green being a popular color. However, I have had success with many different colors associated with spreader bars. If I have learned nothing else during all my years of fishing in the ocean, it is "if what I am doing is not working, try something else!" Which brings us to the next method of catching bluefin: planers.

Using planers often is the ticket to a successful day when fishing for bluefin. As mentioned pervious in the studies, bluefin spend more time 50' or deeper in the water column then near the surface. It only makes sense for anglers to place their baits in that vicinity to enhance bites, and planers are a good way to accomplish this. See chapter 6 for information on how to rig planers. The best planer rig for bluefin is probably dedicating a planer rod and using the removable planer system. Keep the bait 100' from the planer, as this distance seems to make a difference in the amount of fish caught. Black and purple skirts over ballyhoo are a good choice, as is a pink skirted ballyhoo if not run too deep. Of course the old standard, a number 3-½ drone spoon, can be counted on to take its fair share of bluefin as well.

I've certainly caught my fair share of bluefin while trolling, but undoubtedly chunking has been my most productive method for constantly taking large bluefin. The key to chunking for bluefin tuna is deep lines. Do not get me wrong, they will take suspended baits and hand-fed lines. However, baits fish just off the bottom have accounted for more 200-pound bluefin tuna for my charters than those fished in any other location. Fish one line just off the bottom underneath the boat, and at least one additional line suspended under a float near the bottom. While butterfish is probably the number one chunking bait in the Mid Atlantic, I have found rigged whole squid also very successful in hooking up bluefin. Another trick for catching bluefin, especially when the current is running, is to freespool a line set

The author displays a good eating-size yellowfin.

under the thermocline at 60'. By freespooling the line, the bait appears natural drifting along with the current. Drift the line 250 to 300 yards, wind it back in, and repeat. As with yellowfin, I recommend the use of fluorocarbon leaders. Bluefin do not appear to be as leery of leader as yellowfin, but fluorocarbon certainly will increase your hookup percentage.

TUNA — YELLOWFIN

Yellowfin tuna are without a doubt the bread and butter of the charter fishing fleets from the Carolinas north to Massachusetts. They are also the number one reason recreational anglers leave port each day, heading east. Anglers may seek out white marlin, blue marlin, or dolphin, but in the back of the fishermen's minds they always have high hopes for putting yellowfin in the box. To increase the chances of success, it will be beneficial to understand a little about yellowfin tuna.

Yellowfin tuna grow rapidly and have a shorter life span than other tunas. This may be one reason that they have been able to withstand high fishing pressure from both the commercial and recreational end. Yellowfin achieve a weight of eight to 10 pounds during their first year of life. At age two they tip the scales somewhere around 35 pounds, and reach 75 pounds by around age three. Sexual maturity is reached somewhere between age two and three. Yellowfin grow in excess of 200 pounds, but along the Atlantic seaboard catches exceeding 100 pounds are rare and noteworthy.

Identifying the yellowfin tuna, or Thunnus albacares, from its other cousins can be difficult. Newcomers to offshore fishing often find yellowfin and bluefin difficult to tell apart. Many, many, many decades ago, my uncle and I had a discussion concerning all the tuna laying about the dock. Since they all had yellowfin fins, I thought they were yellowfin. Of course, I was wrong. To my dismay, they were bluefin—and thus a learning experiences. The easiest way to identify a yellowfin is by looking at the pectoral fin. If you draw an imaginary vertical line across the tuna beginning at the front of the second dorsal fin, the pectoral fin comes to this line. The pectoral fin on a longfin (albacore) extends well beyond the second dorsal fin. The bluefin pectoral fins fall well short of the second dorsal fin. The yellowfin tuna also tends to be slightly more streamlined then a bluefin, although to a novice, this is not an identifiable feature. Another telltale sign to distinguish the difference between a bluefin and yellowfin comes during the battle. If the angler observes the fish when hooked near the boat, the pectoral fins appear as airplane wings stretched out. The bluefin tends to keep the fins closer to its body.

The yellowfin's circulatory system acts to retain heat in a way similar to the bluefin, but not to the same degree. This allows their bodies to maintain temperatures above the surrounding waters. However, their ability to stay warm does not come near that of the bluefin tuna and as a result, they tend to limit vertical movement and stay above the thermocline. This does not mean they will not or do not feed near the bottom when on inshore lumps along the 30 fathom line. But, anglers concentrating fishing efforts above the thermocline often find the best success. Yellowfin may be found migrating in water as low as 64 degrees, but normally do not take up residence until the water is 68 or higher.

The number one method of catching yellowfin is by trolling. A typical spread consisting of flat lines, short riggers and long riggers, and often a shotgun, (or "way back" line) produces fish. Artificial or rigged natural baits are both equally up to the task of attracting yellowfin to the back of the boat. Spreader bars are especially adapted to catching yellowfin. Often, multiple hookups are possible if the boat maintains forward momentum after the first fish is hooked.

Many times yellowfin are hesitant to rise to the surface in order to feed. On these days, anglers may find a rigged ballyhoo with a pink skirt pulled on a downrigger or a planer just the trick for putting fish in the box. When yellowfin tuna are concentrated on lumps, there is no better method for catching them then chunking. Being a school fish, they are very susceptible to this type of fishing. It is difficult to deceive a yellowfin's eyesight, however. Make sure the hook is completely concealed in the butterfish or whatever bait is being used. Whether to use fluorocarbon or not is not even up for discussion. However, there is room to quibble over the leader poundage. Fluorocarbon is not invisible, and bright sunny days with crystal clear water create conditions where tuna become leader shy. Then for some unknown reason, there are days it appears line diameter makes absolutely no difference. But, make no mistake, these days are far and few between. Just to be on the safe side, fluorocarbon is always recommended. Start with the lightest leader you feel comfortable using. I begin with 50-pound test, if necessary dropping down to 30. I have observed tuna shying away from 50-pound test fluorocarbon when the water is clear and a bright sun high in the sky. One day 18-pound fluorocarbon was necessary in order for the yellowfin to pick up the bait. We did not manage to put many in the box, but at least it accounted for hookups and excitement. Since light leader does not allow wiring a fish, never make a leader more than six foot in length or you will not be able to gaff the fish.

Setting lines consist of suspending baits at various depths that correspond with the chunk line. The chunk rate of descent will vary day to day depending on the current. Lines consist of floaters with no weight, right behind the boat, to lines set at depths of 100' or more. Use appropriate size egg sinkers for weight. Slide the sinker at least 20' up the line above the swivel and hold it in place with a rubber band. Anywhere from ¼ to six ounces of lead is normally sufficient depending on the current. However, occasionally there will be strong current below the thermocline making heavier weight necessary. A trick when using a floater line is to hand-feed the fish. Free spool the line and allow it to drift back along with the chunks. Many times yellowfin tuna are hesitant to pick up bait that does not appear natural in water, and this trick has accounted for many tuna on slow days. Cut butterfish into five or six pieces and begin chunking by throwing a piece spaced out about every five or six feet. Throw a handful in for good measure every now and then. Once you have the fish behind the boat it is imperative that you do not stop chunking. Often the chum line is stopped or broken during confusion or excitement in the pit while fish are being caught. Everyone has a job, and someone must continue to throw chunk to keep fish behind the boat. This is especially important when there are multiple hookups—someone must keep the chunk flowing. Otherwise, the school will move on in search of more food. There is nothing more frustrating than catching one fish, only to lose the school and watch another boat fishing in the same area catch the rest of "your" fish.

Circle hooks in a 9/0 to 11/0 size are ideal for chunking and produce a better hook up percentage J hooks. In addition, circle hooks allow a fish to be hooked with the rod in the holder. How to set the drag is a matter of personal preference. When fish are extremely finicky, the drag must be set extremely light or they often drop the bait as soon as pressure is felt. Then there are days when the drag can be set in strike position with six to eight pounds of pressure. In this manner, the fish automatically hook themselves when a line comes tight. I begin by setting the drag into strike position, only changing to an extremely light drag when necessary.

Normally, if you find bait you will find fish. I am uncertain how long tuna stay on a lump or edge. Since tuna must constantly keep swimming, they probably are constantly on the move from area to area. However, when baitfish stay in the general area, it is my opinion that schools of pelagic yellowfin come and go on a regular basis as they migrate up and down the coast.

Another trick while chunking is to dangle a diamond jig off of an outrigger. The rocking motion from the boat keeps the jig moving up and down and often can account for an extra fish or two. Watch the fish finder and place the jig at the depth were most of the fish or baits are being observed. Off the Jersey shore, it is very common to use jigs for yellowfin tuna. If tuna are being marked deep and refuse to come to the surface, then sometimes a jig can be your best bet for hooking up yellowfin.

No wonder angler Charlie Cooke is smiling—the wahoo is a connoisseur's delight.

WAHOO

Known as Acanthocybium solandri to the scientific community, ono to those fishing Hawaiian waters or wahoo here along the Atlantic seaboard, any angler who has tangled with this fish has tagged it the fastest swimmer in the ocean. Those that target sailfish may argue this point, and with good reason since both fish are capable of screaming line off the reel at near 60-mph. However, the strike of these sleek speedsters sets them apart. Sailfish may fool around with a bait before the bite, but this is not the case with a wahoo, who likes to eat on the run. When this fish wants to go supersonic, it is able to fold the dorsal fin into a slot in the back, making it more streamlined for speed.

I have never spoken to an angler nor captain that did not get excited about hooking and landing a wahoo. They take a bait and make runs that are breathtaking. As table fare, they are a connoisseur's delight. The meat is snowy white, firm in texture, and very mild tasting. In addition, it freezes very well. In short, it is my favorite fish on the dinner table. I find it far superior to tuna or dolphin! Yet few anglers specifically pull out of the slip each day targeting them. Further more, wahoo are not heavily sought after commercially so they are not under a lot of fishing pressure.

Wahoo are a pelagic fish residing near the continental shelf and are rarely found inshore in dirty green waters. There is only one fish which wahoo may be confused with, their cousin the kingfish. However, upon close inspection, they're easily distinguishable from kings. When first taken out of the water, wahoo have vertical bands which are missing on kings. But these disappear shortly after being removed from the water, which sometimes creates confusion if they are not immediately identified.

Found as far north as New Jersey, they range south along the Atlantic coast. As with most pelagic species, they follow warm water and migrate north in summer and south in winter. Biologist studying stomach content have identified flying fish, ballyhoo, squid, small tuna, and bonito as the most common meals. A common feeding tactic when attacking larger fish is to shear off the tail, then return to finish off the prey.

Wahoo are not school fish, but roam as loners. Yet, they do appear to feed in packs at times. It is difficult to constantly locate them and produce hookups. Wahoo average 30 to 40 pounds, however 60- to 80-pound fish are not uncommon.

Unless you dedicate a rig to specifically catch wahoo, the chances of success are slim. Their razor sharp teeth are capable of cutting through monofilament like a hot knife through butter. To increase your chances of success, dedicate a 50 class outfit in your spread for wahoo. It may appear ludicrous to think a wahoo will be attracted one line over another. However, they do appear to be partial to certain colors.

Before we get into the nuts and bolts of catching wahoo, let's set the rod up. As I have mentioned, wahoo teeth are the first concern when rigging. Set the rod up using a six-foot piece of 80- to100-pound single-strand wire leader. Use a haywire twist and install a 100-pound Spro swivel. This is attached to the fishing line. Rig natural baits such as ballyhoo or mullet on the wire leader, as per the recommendations in the rigging section. If you're using a large artificial where the teeth cannot reach the leader, the wire can be eliminated.

Wahoo will attack just about any size or type of bait. However, color does make a difference. 75-percent of the wahoo I have caught attacked a black/purple or black/red combo. Dark colored morning trolling spreads are normally changed over to lighter colors as the sun rises in the sky. This is not the case with the wahoo rod. Keep the dark color scheme regardless of light conditions. Who knows, this may account for the hookups on this rod during the day, since this rig calls attention for being the odd color.

— CHAPTER ELEVEN —
FORECASTING WEATHER

Mother Nature has a twisted sense of humor. She can take a beautiful, clear blue sky and ruin it when your back is turned. Do not let changing weather catch you by surprise. Most fishermen including myself have come to the conclusion that meteorologist are very efficient at forecasting marine weather for a time frame of about 10 minutes. Outside of this, your guess may be as accurate as the weatherman's. Okay, I may be exaggerating, but you get the point. Learning how to identify upcoming weather based on current conditions is an art that has all but fallen by the wayside. Fishermen have come to depend solely upon marine weather forecasts. Weather satellite information combined with weather predictions is a great asset. However, old seasoned captains could tell impending weather by looking at the type of clouds, wind direction and the condition of a barometer. Since nothing changes like the weather, the following guidelines can give you a heads-up while fishing and watching the sky.

**An unexpected weather front can
ruin a good day of fishing.**

WEATHER SAYINGS

Old weather sayings may not always be accurate. However, they have been passed down over generations and used as a rule of thumb for predicting the weather. Here are a few of the well know quips and the wisdom behind them.

• Red sky in the morning, sailors take warning; Red sky at night, sailors delight.

In the Northern Hemisphere, weather normally moves from west to east. The color of the horizon is caused by dust and other particles in the atmosphere and is associated with nice weather. This means a red sky in the morning (looking to the east) means dry weather has passed with wet weather coming. A red sky at night (looking west) indicated dry weather is coming your way.

• Mackerel sky and mares' tails make lofty ships carry low sails.

"Mackerel" sky, which are cirrocumulus clouds, and "mares' tails," being cirrus clouds, indicate that moisture is in the air and wet weather is in the near future.

• The higher the clouds the better the weather.

High clouds indicate the presence of dry air and high pressure, meaning fair weather.

• Rainbow to windward, foul fall the day; rainbow to leeward, rain runs away.

When the wind blows from the direction of the rainbow, rain is heading towards you. If the rain is downwind, then it has already passed you by.

• A wind from the south has rain in its mouth.

A south wind blows in advance of a cold front. It also blows over the east quadrant of an approaching low-pressure system. Meaning, rain is coming.

• Sea gull, sea gull, sit on the sand; it's a sign of rain when you are at hand.

Birds tend to roost more during periods of low pressure. If you live along the east coast, you will notice them inshore hanging around parking lots when bad weather is on the way.

HOW WEATHER AFFECTS THE BITE

Weather does more then play a role as the deciding factor of whether it is safe enough to venture offshore to participate in our favorite past time. Its effect on our quarry should also be taken in account. Water temperature, currents, clarity, number of boats fishing an area, moon phase, the list of what affects fish and their decision to cooperate with us goes on and on. However, possibly nothing can open the mouth of a fish more then the weather. Time and time again weather has been patterned to coincide with the bite. Anglers fish when opportunity exists. Nonetheless, when a choice of fishing days is possible, take the following into consideration.

BAROMETRIC PRESSURE

Barometric pressure is measured by a barometer, which weighs the pressure of the atmosphere per square inch against the weight of mercury. The first prototype mercury barometer was actually constructed in 1643 by Evangelista Torricelli and his student, Vincenzo Viviani. To my knowledge, neither was a fisherman nor knew the true importance of their discovery! But, it would take until 1843, when Lucien Vidie, a French scientist made the first working version of the Aneroid (meaning "without liquid") barometer. Without worry of mercury spillage, barometers could then be used on ships by mariners to foretell weather changes. Today, new electronic sensors used with microprocessor chips have replaced the aneroid cells.

What is the importance of barometric pressure? It tells us the amount of atmosphere pressure exerted on water, which in turn appears to have an effect on the feeding habits of fish.

Understanding barometric pressure is pretty simplistic if one does not dig to deep into the subject. It changes when weather systems, good or foul, come our way. On weather maps, H stands for high pressure and L for low pressure. High pressure is associated with good weather, while low pressure means foul. High pressure is measured around 30.50" with low pressure down around 29.00", depending on the strength of the pressure systems. For fishing purposes, it is the changing of the barometer that appears to open the mouths of fish. This means as a high or low pressure system leaves or comes into your area, chances of catching fish improve.

These following rules are not carved into stone, but more often then not they are correct and worth attention.

• High barometric pressure - Fish tend to be lock jawed and seek deeper water. High pressure is associated with clear skies and nice weather.

• Rising barometer - Decent fishing, fish are fairly active. Weather condition is clearing or improving.

• Stable barometer, around 30" of pressure - Normal fishing. Weather is fair.

• Falling barometer - Most active period for fish. Fishing can be fantastic for a period of time before the low pressure front sets in. This can be the best time to fish according to the barometric pressure, but, it can be one of the worst times to be on the ocean because of the accompanying deteriorating weather. Venture offshore with caution.

• Slightly lower barometer - Fishing can be good. Many times fish are aggressive. This is probably due to the sky, which is normally overcast. Fish tend to rise towards the surface to feed with the lack of sunlight.

• Low barometer - Fish become less active and lock-jawed. Weather is rainy and stormy. A great time to make new rigs!

Of course, there is a simpler way to judge the bite and if the weather will co-operate by remembering this old saying:

• Wind from the west, fish bite the best; wind from the east, fish bite the least; wind from the north, do not go forth; wind from the south blows bait in their mouth!

— CHAPTER TWELVE —
END OF THE LINE!

This book ends where your fishing begins! I trust every reader learned valuable information to increase their offshore fishing ability. Keep in mind, once fish are caught the best is yet to come—dining on the freshest catch possible. The flavor of fish cannot be made better then when they are first removed from the water. All an angler can hope for is to reduce the rate of meat deterioration. Proper attention to the catch is imperative if your palate is to experience the incomparable taste that fresh fish offers on the table.

There is one word to remember for preserving your catch: ICE. Dress large pelagic species by removing the stomach and pack the body cavity with ice. This quickly cools down the inside of the fish and really helps to preserve freshness. Keep in mind, species like tuna are under regulations concerning removal of the head at sea. In short, the regulation states anglers may not remove the head of yellowfin or bigeye if the remaining section of the fish is less then 27". There is a conversion factor for bluefin that allows a bluefin to be 20" (at the present time; remember that these rules can change season to season) without the head. To avoid running into a problem, I recommend leaving the head intact while at sea.

The gentle handling of fish reduces bruising that distracts from flavor. Try to avoid fish flopping on the deck or thrashing around and striking items in the cockpit. A wet rag thrown over the head of most fish quiets them down until they can be placed carefully in the kill box. This applies to small fish as well as large. The excitement of catching many small fish often ends in throwing the fish into the kill box, instead of carefully placing the fish on ice. For recipes, cleaning and fish handling techniques, I recommend reading "Off the Hook, Rudow's recipes for cooking your catch" by Lenny Rudow. The book contains excellent recipes and recommendations for handling your catch.

As you certainly have realized by this point, I practice conservation and urge all anglers to do the same to help preserve our fisheries. Exercise catch and release after taking what is necessary for consumption. A camera on the boat preserves memories while allowing the fish to provide enjoyment for other anglers in the future.

I close with these final thoughts. Keep records! Record locations fished, water temperature, weather conditions, bait used and any other bit of information that impact fishing each and every day you are lucky enough to be offshore enjoying all that nature has to offer. **Offshore fishing is not**

a science, but an experience in learning! I welcome your comments and catch photos. Send them to OffshorePursuit@aol.com.

See you Offshore!
John W. Unkart

ABOUT THE AUTHOR

John Unkart's childhood memories are mostly of fishing. To say, "he fished before he walked" is not very far from the truth. His father was a sportsman who had a passion for the outdoors. He passed these loves onto John at a very tender age.

John has taken his years of offshore fishing experience and put it to pen in Offshore Pursuit. The beginning chapters of the book explain methods and techniques. This knowledge can then be applied while reading later chapters related to specific species. Chronologically speaking, reading the book from cover to cover presents a learning experience cumulating in knowledge that teaches anglers how to catch fish offshore. John has been blessed with a lifetime of fishing and welcomes this opportunity to share what he has learned over the years.

Tight lines and good fishing!

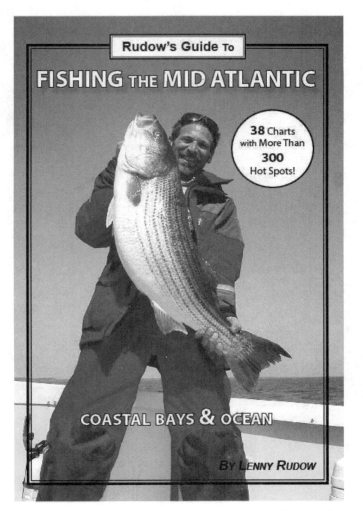

TACTICS, TACKLE, TRICKS, SPREADS, AND RIGGING FOR THE ADVANCED TUNA ANGLER

TUNA FISHING

A MODERN APPROACH FROM THE COCKPIT UP

BY JON MEADE

[ALBACORE * BIGEYE * BLACKFIN * BLUEFIN * YELLOWFIN]

Capt. Jon Meade pours out his knowledge and expertise.
This book details cutting-edge tricks and techniques profes-
sionals use to win big-money tournaments
and put meat in the box.

RUDOW'S GUIDE TO

ROCK FISH

BY LENNY RUDOW

Lenny Rudow's latest how-to/where-to fishing book details the tactics, tackle and techniques used by recreational and professional anglers, and discusses which is most effective.